South Carolina
PACT
Test
Preparation
Book

Grade 4

Harcourt

Orlando   Austin   Chicago   New York   Toronto   London   San Diego

Visit *The Learning Site!*
www.harcourtschool.com

Printed in the United States of America

ISBN 0-15-338382-8

7 8 9 10   073   10 09 08 07

CONTENTS

Tips for Taking a Test 4–7

Theme 1

   Lesson 1 8–11

   Lesson 2 12–15

   Lesson 3 16–19

   Lesson 4 20–23

   Lesson 5 24–26

   Time to Write. 27

Theme 2

   Lesson 6 28–31

   Lesson 7 32–35

   Lesson 8 36–39

   Lesson 9 40–43

   Lesson 10 44–46

   Time to Write. 47

Theme 3

   Lesson 11 48–51

   Lesson 12 52–55

   Lesson 13 56–59

   Lesson 14 60–63

   Lesson 15 64–66

   Time to Write. 67

CONTENTS

Theme 4

Lesson 16 68–71

Lesson 17 72–75

Lesson 18 76–79

Lesson 19 80–83

Lesson 20 84–86

Time to Write 87

Theme 5

Lesson 21 88–91

Lesson 22 92–95

Lesson 23 96–99

Lesson 24 100–103

Lesson 25 104–106

Time to Write 107

Theme 6

Lesson 26 108–111

Lesson 27 112–115

Lesson 28 116–119

Lesson 29 120–123

Lesson 30 124–126

Time to Write 127

Tips for Taking a Test

Preparation

- ✅ Sit quietly.
- ✅ Look at the speaker.
- ✅ Listen for directions.
- ✅ Sit straight and comfortably in your chair.
- ✅ Keep your eyes on the teacher and the test booklet.
- ✅ Have sharpened pencils ready.

Mark It Correctly

Answer choices must be marked carefully when you take a test.

- ◯ Incorrect
- ⊗ Incorrect
- ● Correct
- ◑ Incorrect

Signs Along the Way

While you are taking a test, you should pay attention to the words and directions on the pages. Look at the words in the boxes below. Think about what you should do when you see these words on a test. Then answer the questions.

DIRECTIONS		**STOP**

1 What word or words tell you to read about how to do a test section?

○ GO ON

○ DIRECTIONS

○ STOP

2 What word or words tell you to continue working?

○ GO ON

○ DIRECTIONS

○ STOP

3 What word or words tell you that you have reached the last question in a section?

○ GO ON

○ DIRECTIONS

○ STOP

© Harcourt

Following Directions

When you begin a test section, read the directions carefully, paying attention to words in special type.

Read the information in the left column. Then answer the questions about following directions.

DIRECTIONS

Choose the word or group of words that means the same, or about the same, as the underlined word. Then mark the space for the answer you have chosen.

1 **The underlined word and the answer**

○ have opposite meanings

○ have similar meanings

○ do not have the same meanings

○ are the same word

DIRECTIONS

Read the passage. Then read each question about the passage. Decide which is the best answer to the question. Mark the space for the answer you have chosen.

2 **What should you do after you read the passage?**

○ Answer the most difficult question.

○ Reread the passage.

○ Read the questions.

○ Finish the last section.

DIRECTIONS

Read the sentence, paying attention to the underlined words. There may be a mistake in punctuation, capitalization, or word usage. If you find a mistake, choose the answer that is the best way to write the underlined section of the sentence. If there is no mistake, choose *Correct as is*.

3 **If you do not find an error in the sentence, which answer space should you mark?**

○ Go on

○ Correct as is

○ DIRECTIONS

Read It and Understand

Being alert during a test means watching out for important words that will help you answer questions quickly and accurately. <u>Underlined</u> words, *italic* words, words on their own line, and words in boxes signal important information. Read the information in the left column, and answer the numbered questions on the right.

What is the *main* reason this story was written?

1 What is the important part of this question?

- ○ written
- ○ main
- ○ story
- ○ reason

Something that is <u>perplexing</u> is—

2 What is the important part of this question?

- ○ Something
- ○ that
- ○ perplexing
- ○ is

Everything the colonists did angered King George *except*—

3 What is the important part of this question?

- ○ King George
- ○ colonists
- ○ angered
- ○ except

Look at these guide words from a dictionary page.

almost—apple

Which word can be found on the page?

4 What is the important part of this question?

- ○ almost—apple
- ○ Look
- ○ dictionary page
- ○ guide

Directions

Read the story below. Then answer Questions 1 through 6. You may look back at the story.

Buffalo Grass

Kim was walking to the library when she saw her neighbor Margo in the yard. Margo was writing *For Sale* on a big piece of cardboard. On the sidewalk beside her were a lawn mower, two sprinklers, and four garden hoses.

"Hi, Margo," said Kim. "It looks as if you're having a sale."

"Yes, indeed," said Margo happily. "I'm selling my lawn equipment."

"How will you take care of your lawn?" Kim asked. "Your grass is the prettiest in the neighborhood!"

"I know," said Margo. "It's green because I feed it and water it so much. I've decided that it's wrong for this area. Today, people are bringing me my new buffalo grass."

Kim thought about grass that buffaloes would eat. She imagined a little piece of the Great Plains in Margo's yard. "Are you planting a prairie?" she asked.

"Exactly!" exclaimed Margo. "This is the same grass that settlers used to build sod houses. Buffalo grass can grow without much water. Since it grows only 8 inches tall, I'll mow only a couple of times a year. I'm going to get a mower that I can power myself. Without the loud engine running, I can hear the birds."

"If you're not taking care of your grass, when will I see you?" Kim asked.

Margo laughed. "Do you see those two chairs on the porch? Those chairs are for us to sit in and admire the grass. I'll have more time for relaxing than I have now."

FOR SALE
lawn mower
sprinklers
garden hoses

Tip

Notice that the speaker has changed. Kim speaks in the last paragraph. Margo speaks in this paragraph.

Tip

Try to imagine what a prairie looks like. How do you think it is different from a regular lawn?

© Harcourt

Name _____

1 **Which picture shows the setting of this story?**

○   ○   ○   ○

Tip
Some of these places are mentioned in the story, but only one tells where the story happens.

2 **Margo is selling**

○ a big piece of cardboard.

○ her lawn mower, sprinklers, and hoses.

○ her yard.

○ two chairs on her porch.

3 **Margo's lawn is so green because**

○ she feeds it and waters it so much.

○ it is a new kind of grass.

○ she doesn't mow it.

○ she lives on the prairie.

4 **According to the story, which of these statements is not true about buffalo grass?**

○ It needs to be mowed often.

○ Settlers used it to build sod houses.

○ It grows only 8 inches tall.

○ It needs little water.

Tip
Pay attention to the word *not* in the question. One answer choice gives information that is not true.

5 **The author probably wrote this story to**

○ describe the best way to water a lawn.

○ urge people to mow their lawns more often.

○ tell people about a kind of grass that saves time and water.

○ persuade people to buy lawn mowers.

6 **Write a sentence that tells what change Margo is making in her yard.**

_____

_____

_____

Standards: 4-R2.1, 4-R1.10, 4-R1.10, 4-R1.7, 4-R2.10, 4-R1.4

Directions

Read this paragraph from a composition a student wrote about water. It has several mistakes that need correcting. Then answer Questions 7 through 9.

Water Is Important

[1] Did you ever stop to think that water is necessary for all living things? [2] Plants cannot grow without water. [3] Whether they grow wild, in gardens, or on farms. [4] Animals needs water to drink. [5] people also must have water in order to live.

Tip

A sentence tells a complete thought. It names someone or something and tells what that person or thing is or does.

7 Which statement is _not_ a sentence?

○ Statement 1

○ Statement 2

○ Statement 3

○ Statement 5

8 Which is the _best_ way to rewrite Sentence 4?

Tip

Remember that the verb must agree with its subject.

○ An animal need water to drink.

○ Animals need water to drink.

○ Animals needing water to drink.

○ An animal have needed water to drink.

9 How should the error in Sentence 5 be corrected?

○ by changing the period to a question mark

○ by capitalizing the first word of the sentence

○ by adding a comma after _also_

○ by writing it without an end mark

Standards: 4-W1.5, 4-W1.5, 4-W1.5

GO ON

© Harcourt

Directions

Look at the underlined part of the sentence. Choose the answer that shows the correct punctuation for that part. If the underlined part is correct, mark "Correct as is."

10 The house on the <u>corner. has</u> a beautiful green lawn.

- ○ corner has
- ○ corner? has
- ○ corner, has
- ○ Correct as is

Tip

First, identify a punctuation error in the underlined part of the sentence. Then, decide how to correct it.

11 Read the phrases. Look for an underlined word that is used incorrectly. If the underlined words are used correctly, mark "All correct."

- ○ days of the <u>weak</u>
- ○ <u>ties</u> a shoe
- ○ running <u>fast</u>
- ○ All correct

12 Choose the word that is spelled correctly and completes the sentence.

I enjoy working outdoors with others in my

- ○ famly.
- ○ fammily.
- ○ famelly.
- ○ family.

Standards: 4-W1.5, 4-W1.5, 4-W1.5

STOP

Directions

Read the poem below. Then answer Questions 1 through 6. You may look back at the poem.

On the Interstate

Driving down the interstate,

Hoping we will not be late,

We come to an interchange,

A place where routes may rearrange

Because two highways intersect.

In other words, they interconnect.

Mom says, "Go left." Dad says, "Go right."

We wait an interminable time at the light.

The light was red, but now it's green.

I don't interfere or intervene.

They reach an agreement. They make a decision.

Will we get to the show before intermission?

Tip

Have you noticed that many of the words in this poem have the prefix *inter–*? Look for other prefixes, suffixes, and root words that you know.

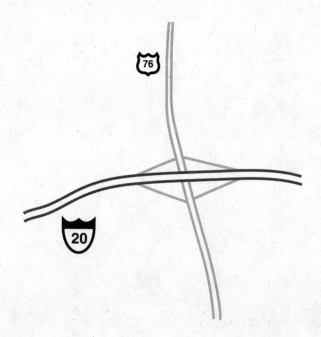

1 The meaning of *intersect* is

○ divide
○ interconnect
○ end
○ begin

Tip
The phrase *in other words* indicates that an author is about to say something a second time but in a different way.

2 Who is the narrator of the poem?

○ the driver of the car
○ a child riding in the family car
○ Dad
○ a highway patrol officer

3 Where are the people in the car going?

○ to a show
○ home
○ to a restaurant
○ The poem does not say.

4 Which word best describes the tone of this poem?

○ serious
○ angry
○ playful
○ uninterested

Tip
Choose the word that best describes the feeling the author conveys by the choice of words and the way the poem is written.

5 Look at the first four lines of the poem. What is the rhyming pattern?

○ Only the first and third lines rhyme.
○ Only the second and fourth lines rhyme.
○ The first and second lines rhyme, and the third and fourth lines rhyme.
○ The first and third lines rhyme, and the second and fourth lines rhyme.

6 Write a sentence or two telling how the drawing helps a reader understand the poem.

_____

_____

_____

Standards: 4-R3.4, 4-R2.3, 4-R1.7, 4-R2.1, 4-R2.9

GO ON

Directions

Read this paragraph from a composition a student wrote. It has several mistakes that need correcting. Then answer Questions 7 through 9.

Building a Bird Feeder

¹ Jeff wanted to make a bird feeder. ² His friend meg tells him how to make a feeder from an empty plastic soda bottle. ³ When the feeder was done, Dad gave Jeff seeds to put in it. ⁴ helped Jeff hang the feeder from the branch of a tree. ⁵ Now Jeff enjoy watching from the window as the birds eat from his feeder.

---

7 How can the error in Statement 4 be corrected?

○ by changing the period to a question mark

○ by changing the small *h* in *helped* to a capital *H*

○ by adding the subject *He* before *helped*

○ by adding a comma after *feeder*

8 Which is the best way to rewrite Sentence 2?

○ His friend meg told him how to make a feeder from an empty plastic soda bottle.

○ His friend Meg tells him how to make a feeder from an empty plastic soda bottle.

○ His friend Meg told him how to make a feeder from an empty plastic soda bottle.

○ His friend meg tells him how to make a feeder from an empty plastic soda bottle?

Tip
Look carefully at Sentence 2. You may find that there is more than one error that needs to be corrected.

9 Which change should be made to correct the error in Sentence 5?

○ Change *Now* to *Know*.

○ Change *Jeff* to *Jeff, he*.

○ Change *enjoy* to *enjoys*.

○ Change *eat* to *eats*.

Standards: 4-W1.5, 4-W1.5, 4-W1.5

GO ON

© Harcourt

Directions

Look at the underlined part of the sentence. Choose the answer that shows the correct punctuation for that part. If the underlined part is correct, mark "Correct as is."

10 Did you see that bright red <u>bird.</u>

○ bird
○ bird?
○ bird,
○ Correct as is

Tip
Think about what end mark is correct for this type of sentence.

11 Read the sentence. Choose the answer that tells which word should be capitalized. If the capitalization is correct, mark "Correct as is."

Mr. henry drove his truck from the city to the lake.

○ henry
○ city
○ lake
○ Correct as is

Tip
Decide whether each choice is a common noun or a proper noun. Proper nouns should be capitalized.

12 Read the phrases. Choose the phrase containing an underlined word that is spelled wrong. If all the underlined words are spelled correctly, mark "All correct."

○ a loud <u>screem</u>
○ a good <u>reason</u>
○ a flock of <u>geese</u>
○ All correct

Standards: 4-W1.5, 4-W1.5, 4-W1.5

STOP

Name _____

Directions

Read the story below. Then answer Questions 1 through 6. You may look back at the story.

An Artful Solution

Our project started with a notice in the school paper about a school art fair. "I want everyone to bring in something for the fair," our teacher said. "You may work in pairs if you like."

Soon everyone else was working on their projects. Only Isaac and I had no ideas. We decided to try our school library. Candlemaking? Flower arranging? Origami? None of these interested us. Then, near the end of the art section, we saw it.

"Hey, Wally, what do you think of these pictures?" Isaac asked me. The cover of the book showed a dressed-up dog. The photographs were by William Wegman.

"These are cool!" I said. Isaac and I decided to be animal photographers. We planned our project and had some wonderful ideas. We would put Samson in a hat and get him to sit still while we took his picture.

Isaac came over the next afternoon. We borrowed a beret from my sister.

"This will look great!" Isaac said.

Well, Samson didn't think so. He shook the hat off his head right away. We decided to try the sunbonnet my parents got in San Diego, California. When I tied the string under his chin, the hat covered Samson's eyes. He shook his head back and forth and barked. My mother told us to leave him alone.

"Why don't you two boys walk around the neighborhood and take some pictures?" she suggested.

So, that's what we did. Our pictures weren't the most exciting ones in the art fair. They didn't win any prizes, but at least Samson enjoyed the rest of his day.

Tip
If you don't know what the word *beret* means, read on to see if there is something later in the story that can help you figure out the meaning.

Name _____

1   The problem faced by the main characters in this story is

   ○ finding partners to work with.

   ○ planning and completing an art project.

   ○ finding a hat for Samson.

   ○ a disagreement with their mothers.

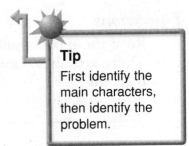

Tip
First identify the main characters, then identify the problem.

2   Here are some events from the story. Place the events in order from 1 to 4 by writing the numbers in the boxes next to each sentence.

   ☐ The boys enter pictures at the art fair.

   ☐ The boys walk around the neighborhood.

   ☐ The boys go to the library.

   ☐ The boys try to take pictures of Samson.

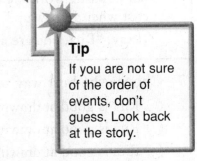

Tip
If you are not sure of the order of events, don't guess. Look back at the story.

3   Samson is probably

   ○ Wally's sister.

   ○ a classmate.

   ○ a dog.

   ○ a visitor from California.

4   The meaning of the word _beret_ in this story is

   ○ a hat.

   ○ a scarf.

   ○ a head.

   ○ a string.

5   Samson enjoyed the rest of his day because

   ○ he had a new hat to wear.

   ○ the boys took his picture.

   ○ he got to go for a walk.

   ○ no one was trying to dress him up.

6   Should an animal be dressed in clothes for a photograph? Write a sentence giving your opinion. Then write another sentence in which you support your opinion.

   _____

   _____

   _____

Standards: 4-R2.2, 4-R2.1, 4-R1.10, 4-R3.4, 4-R1.10, 4-R1.16

17

GO ON

Directions

Read these paragraphs from a composition a student wrote about a friend. There are several mistakes that need correcting. Then answer Questions 7 through 9.

The Artist

¹ Rita is good at drawing. ² Rita is good at painting.

³ What fantastic work she does? ⁴ She say, "I want to be an artist when I grow up."

⁵ I say, "Rita, you are an artist already!"

---

7 Choose the <u>best</u> way to combine Sentences 1 and 2.

○ Rita is good at drawing, Rita is good at painting.

○ Rita is good at drawing, and Rita is good at painting.

○ Rita is good at drawing and painting.

○ Rita are good at drawing and painting.

8 Sentence 3 should end with _____ instead of a question mark.

○ a period

○ a comma

○ a semicolon

○ an exclamation point

Tip
Reread Sentence 3 to decide what type of sentence it is. Choose the end mark that is correct for this type of sentence.

9 How can the error in Sentence 4 be corrected?

○ by changing *say* to *says*

○ by changing *want* to *wants*

○ by changing *an* to *a*

○ by changing the period to a question mark

© Harcourt

---

*D*irections

Read the sentence. Choose the answer that shows
which words in the sentence should be capitalized.
If the capitalization is correct, mark "Correct as is."

10 My brother ed and i go to the same school.

○ My brother ed and I go to the same school.
○ My brother Ed and I go to the same school.
○ My Brother Ed and I go to the same School.
○ Correct as is

11 Which word <u>best</u> completes the analogy?

Connect is to *join* as *fracture* is to _____ .

○ break
○ fix
○ erase
○ close

12 Choose the word that is spelled correctly and
completes the sentence.

Everyone _____ **to the window to see what was
happening.**

○ hurryed
○ hurried
○ hurreyd
○ hurreied

Tip
First think of how
to spell the root
word. Then recall
how the spelling
changes when the
-ed ending is
added.

*D*irections

Read the article below. Then answer Questions 1 through 5.
You may look back at the article.

Cyclocross

Do you like to get out in the country and enjoy nature?
Do you like to ride a bike? If so, you should try racing in an
event called cyclocross. In this sport, you have to ride your
bike, *and* you have to carry it!

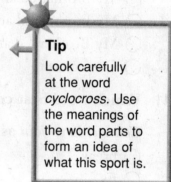

Tip
Look carefully
at the word
cyclocross. Use
the meanings of
the word parts to
form an idea of
what this sport is.

You spend only part of the race on your bike because only
half of the course is smooth. The other half goes through
country fields. Bikers travel through areas filled with logs,
sandpits, mud puddles, fences, and piles of wood. Several
times during the race, riders hop off their bikes, hang them
over their shoulders, and run as fast as they can while
carrying their bikes.

Deciding when to ride and when to run is part of a racer's
strategy. At some points, however, barricades or hurdles are
set up to force riders to get off their bikes. These barricades
are 10 to 15 inches high and set close together. While
running with their bikes on their shoulders, the racers also
have to jump over the barricades. As you can imagine, you
must be a strong athlete with good skills to compete in this
sport!

Cyclocross began in Europe about ten years ago as a way for
cyclists to stay fit during the winter. The sport helps bike
riders develop their skills, strength, and endurance.

A cyclocross race usually takes one hour from start to finish.
If you work out an hour a day, three or four days a week,
you'll probably be strong enough to compete in one. You will
need to do some uphill running and exercises that build
muscles in your lower back, stomach, and legs. Check out
sports magazines or do a computer search for more
information about cyclocross. It's a great way to see the
countryside while having fun.

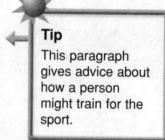

Tip
This paragraph
gives advice about
how a person
might train for the
sport.

1 Which meaning of the root word *cross* is combined with *cyclo* to form the name of the sport?

○ bad-tempered

○ to meet and pass on the way

○ to draw a line through something

○ to move across or over a distance

2 Suppose you have read only the title of this article. Use the title to write a question that the article would probably answer.

_____

_____

_____

3 Which picture shows an obstacle you would probably **not** come upon in a cyclocross race?

○

○

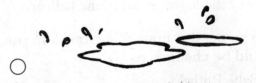

○

4 Which statement is an opinion about cyclocross?

○ The sport began in Europe.

○ Cyclocross is a great way to see the countryside.

○ Riders carry their bikes on their shoulders.

○ Barricades are 10 to 15 inches high.

5 Which of these headings **best** states the main idea of the last paragraph of the article?

○ More Facts About Cyclocross

○ Exercises for Fun and Fitness

○ Getting Ready for Cyclocross

○ How to See the Countryside

Standards: 4-R3.3, 4-RS1.2, 4-R1.6, 4-R1.13, 4-R1.9

GO ON

Directions

Read this paragraph. Then answer Questions 6 through 8.

An Incomparable Player

[1] Henry Aaron was born in Alabama in 1934, the same year that the great Babe Ruth ended Babe Ruth's baseball career with the New York Yankees. [2] Babe Ruth had hit 714 home runs, a record that stood for forty years. [3] It was Henry Aaron who broke that record when he hit home run number 715 on April 8, 1974. [4] Aaron also holds the major league record for runs batted in.

---

6 Which sentence below would be the best closing sentence for the paragraph?

○ Babe Ruth was a great baseball player.

○ Baseball is a popular sport in other parts of the world, as well as in the United States.

○ In 1982, Henry Aaron was elected to the National Baseball Hall of Fame.

○ A home run usually means that the batter hits the ball over the fence or out of the ballpark.

Tip
Think about the main idea of the paragraph and how the text is structured. Pick the answer that tells more about the main idea and fits the structure of the paragraph.

7 The possessive noun *Babe Ruth's* in the first sentence should be changed to

○ Babe Ruths'

○ Henry Aaron's

○ his

○ their

8 Where would this sentence best fit in the paragraph?

He went on to hit a total of 755 home runs.

○ before Sentence 1

○ before Sentence 2

○ before Sentence 3

○ before Sentence 4

Tip
Try rereading the paragraph with the new sentence in each position. Think about where the sentence fits best into the sequence of events.

© Harcourt

Standards: 4-W1.3, 4-W1.5, 4-W1.4

Directions

Read the sentence. Choose the correct verb form to complete the sentence.

9 My sister _____ first base on her Little League team.

○ playing
○ plays
○ player
○ play

Tip
First identify the subject. Decide whether it names one person, place, or thing or more than one. Then choose the verb form that goes with that number.

10 Read the phrases. Look for an underlined word that is used incorrectly. If the underlined words are used correctly, mark "All correct."

○ over <u>there</u>
○ in <u>it's</u> place
○ a <u>new</u> bicycle
○ All correct

11 Choose the word that is spelled correctly and completes the sentence.

We often ask our friends to eat _____ with us.

○ diner
○ dinor
○ dinner
○ dinnar

12 Revise this sentence: *Sports are fun.* Make the language more precise.

_____

_____

_____

Standards: 4-W1.5, 4-W1.5, 4-W1.5, 4-W1.4

STOP

Directions

Read the article below. Then answer Questions 1 through 5. You may look back at the article.

Clara Barton

Clara Barton was born in 1821 in Massachusetts. She was a bright and independent child, though somewhat shy. As she grew older, she discovered that she enjoyed nursing the sick and helping people in need.

The Civil War

In 1861, when the Civil War broke out, Clara Barton went to work helping wounded soldiers. She made nutritious meals from limited supplies, comforted the patients, made sure they had water, and assisted the surgeons in dangerous battlefield conditions. Clara did it all, and she did it well.

After the Civil War ended, Clara Barton gave public talks about her experiences. This was a time before movies, radio, or television. For entertainment, many people went to a public hall to hear speakers tell about interesting events. Clara Barton's talks were popular. Before long, her heroism and hard work on the battlefields became known throughout the country.

The Red Cross

In 1869, while visiting Switzerland, Clara Barton learned about the Red Cross. She set out to start an American branch of this organization that would help people in times of war and disasters. In 1881, as a result of her efforts, the American Red Cross became a reality.

Clara Barton headed the American Red Cross until she was 82 years old. Monuments honoring her work during the war and her life of service can be seen at Antietam National Battlefield and at her home in Glen Echo, Maryland.

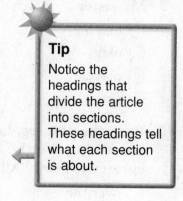

Tip

Notice the headings that divide the article into sections. These headings tell what each section is about.

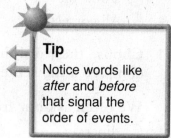

Tip

Notice words like *after* and *before* that signal the order of events.

© Harcourt

Name _____

1 **What is the genre of this text?**
   ○ fiction
   ○ poetry
   ○ drama
   ○ nonfiction

2 **What two topics does this text focus on?**
   ○ Clara Barton's childhood and her involvement in the Civil War
   ○ Clara Barton's involvement in the Civil War and her public talks
   ○ Clara Barton's work during the Civil War and with the American Red Cross
   ○ Clara Barton's work with the American Red Cross and the monuments to her life

Tip
Scanning subheads can help you identify the main focuses of an article.

3 **The article gives enough information for you to conclude that Clara Barton**
   ○ enjoyed public speaking more than she enjoyed helping others.
   ○ loved to travel.
   ○ was deeply affected by her experiences during the Civil War.
   ○ was sorry for many of her actions.

4 **Which part of a textbook would be most helpful for locating information about the Antietam National Battlefield?**
   ○ the title
   ○ the index
   ○ the chapter headings
   ○ the glossary

Tip
Both an index and a list of chapter headings can help you find information in a textbook. An index lists many more topics and has its listings arranged alphabetically.

5 **Write a sentence that tells the author's purpose for writing this article.**

   _____

   _____

   _____

Standards: 4-R2.8, 4-R1.9, 4-R1.10, 4-RS2.1, 4-R2.10

GO ON

Directions

Look at the underlined part of the sentence. Choose the answer that shows the correct punctuation for that part. If the underlined part is correct, mark "Correct as is."

6 We thought we were lost in the <u>woods we</u> used a compass to find our way.

○ woods, we

○ woods. We

○ woods. we

○ Correct as is

Tip

Can you identify more than one complete thought? Decide whether the example is a run-on sentence that should be written as two separate sentences.

7 Read the sentence. Then choose the answer in which the word *fine* has the same meaning as it does in the sentence.

When the time on the parking meter expired, I got a ticket and had to pay a <u>fine</u>.

○ feeling fine

○ reading fine print

○ fine weather

○ a fine for overdue books

Tip

Notice that *fine* is used as a noun in the sentence. Eliminate phrases in which *fine* is not used as a noun.

8 Read the phrases. Choose the phrase containing an underlined word that is spelled wrong. If all the underlined words are spelled correctly, mark "All correct."

○ a red <u>balloon</u>

○ a large <u>group</u>

○ a bowl of <u>fruit</u>

○ All correct

9 Which would be the best resource to find synonyms for the word *woods*?

○ glossary

○ encyclopedia

○ thesaurus

○ dictionary

Standards: 4-W1.5, 4-R3.4, 4-W1.5, 4-R3.1

Time to Write

Directions

Think about a time when you were proud of something that you accomplished. Write a narrative about the experience. Make a plan before you begin writing. Include details about the events leading up to the accomplishment.

Writer's Checklist

Remember to:

❏ Be sure your narrative has a clear beginning, middle, and ending.

❏ Tell the story in your own voice, using the pronoun *I*.

❏ Tell about the events leading up to the accomplishment in the order in which they happened.

❏ Include interesting descriptive words and details.

❏ Organize your narrative into paragraphs.

❏ Include different types of sentences.

❏ Use complete sentences.

❏ Begin sentences and names of people with capital letters.

❏ End every sentence with an end mark.

❏ Check to see that you have spelled each word correctly.

© Harcourt

Directions

Read the play below. Then answer Questions 1 through 5. You may look back at the play.

Who Paid?

A Tale from Turkey

CHARACTERS

Poor Man   Innkeeper

Hodja, *a judge*   Villagers

SETTING: *A courtyard in an old town.*

AT RISE: *The innkeeper is standing in the doorway of his inn. A poor man dressed in rags approaches.*

POOR MAN: Good morning. Can you spare me some soup?

INNKEEPER: (*Impatiently.*) No, I cannot. (*He goes inside.*)

POOR MAN: (*Calling after him.*) Good day then, and may you be well. (*He starts to walk away, then stops and sniffs.*) I smell something cooking. My, it smells good.

INNKEEPER: (*Rushing out.*) Did you steal some of my soup?

POOR MAN: No, sir. I was only smelling the delicious aroma.

INNKEEPER: Then you must pay for the smell! (*To villagers.*) Call the judge! (*A villager leaves and returns with Hodja.*)

HODJA: What is your complaint, Innkeeper?

INNKEEPER: Hodja, I caught this man smelling my soup!

HODJA: So you want to be paid for the smell of your soup? (*Innkeeper nods eagerly.*) I shall pay you myself. (*He takes two gold coins from his pocket and strikes them together to make a loud ringing sound.*) I have paid for the smell of your soup with the sound of my money. Now please be on your way. (*Villagers cheer.*)

Tip

Stage directions are in parentheses and printed in slanted type. They help you understand the actions of the play by telling how characters speak and what they do.

Tip

If you do not remember who *Hodja* is, look back at the list of characters at the beginning of the play.

© Harcourt

1 **The AT RISE section tells you**

○ who the characters are.

○ who is speaking.

○ what is happening as the play begins.

○ where the play takes place.

Tip

If you don't recall the purpose of the AT RISE section, go back and reread it.

2 **Which word is a synonym for *aroma*?**

○ scent

○ soup

○ sniff

○ money

Tip

If this word is not familiar, look back at the play to see how it is used. The context can help you understand its meaning.

3 **Which word best describes the innkeeper in this play?**

○ greedy

○ honest

○ unintelligent

○ cheerful

4 **The two things that Hodja compares are**

○ the sound of eating soup with the sound of money clinking together.

○ the smell of soup cooking with the sound of coins clinking together.

○ the smell of soup cooking with the taste of soup.

○ the sound of coins with the sound of the villagers cheering.

Tip

Read each answer choice carefully. Some of them are very similar. Be sure that both parts of the answer are correct before you mark your choice.

5 **Early in the play, why does the poor man stop and sniff?**

_____

_____

_____

_____

© Harcourt

Standards: 4-R2.8, 4-R3.4, 4-R2.1, 4-R2.11, 4-R.10

Directions

Read this story that a student wrote. It has several mistakes that need correcting. Then answer Questions 6 through 8.

Cookie Crumbles

[1] One stormy night, Antonio and Maya were making cookies. [2] They had just finished mixing the cookie dough suddenly the lights went out. [3] Without electricity, they could not bake no cookies.

[4] "Oh well," said Maya. [5] "That's the way the cookie crumbles."

---

6 **Which sentence contains two complete thoughts and should be written as two sentences?**

○ Sentence 1

○ Sentence 2

○ Sentence 3

○ Sentence 4

7 **Which is the best way to rewrite Sentence 3?**

○ Without electricity, they can't bake no cookies.

○ Without electricity, they could bake their cookies.

○ Without electricity, they could not bake their cookies.

○ Without electricity, neither of them could bake no cookies.

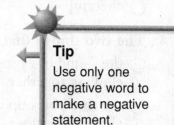

Tip
Use only one negative word to make a negative statement.

8 **How else could Sentence 5 be written and still be correct?**

○ "That's the way the cookie crumbles".

○ "That's the way the cookie crumbles!"

○ "That's the way the cookie crumbles,"

○ "That's the way the cookie crumbles?"

© Harcourt

*D*irections

Read the sentence. Choose the answer that shows which word in the sentence should be capitalized. If the capitalization is correct, mark "Correct as is."

9 The cook at the Fireside restaurant makes great vegetable soup.

○ cook

○ restaurant

○ vegetable

○ Correct as is

Tip

Remember that a proper noun names a particular person, place, or thing. Each important word of a proper noun should begin with a capital letter.

10 Choose the word or words that correctly complete the sentence.

Now I _____ helping my parents in the kitchen.

○ enjoys

○ enjoying

○ enjoy

○ has enjoyed

11 Choose the word that is spelled correctly and completes the sentence.

A _____ uses tools such as a hammer and nails.

○ carpenter

○ carpinter

○ carrpenter

○ carepenter

12 Write three sentences about your favorite food. Explain why you like it.

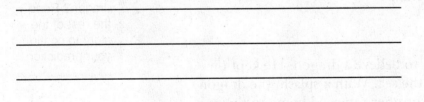

_____

_____

_____

_____

Standards: 4-W1.5, 4-W1.5, 4-W1.5, 4-W2.1

STOP

Name _____

*D*irections

Read the folktale below. Then answer Questions 1 through 5. You may look back at the story.

The Golden Reed Pipe
A Folktale from China

Long ago in China, there lived a woman and her daughter. The daughter was called Little Red because she loved red clothing. One day, a dragon swooped down and carried Little Red away. Her mother heard Little Red's voice crying:

Oh mother, oh mother, as dear as can be.
My brother, my brother will rescue me!

The poor mother did not know what to think, as she had no son. Then one day she found a lost little boy under a bright red berry plant. She named him Redberry.

Redberry was outside when he heard a crow cry:

You have a sister out there, out there!
Save her from the dragon's lair!

Redberry ran to his mother, who told him about Little Red and what had happened. So the boy set out to rescue his sister. He walked until he came to a large rock. He rolled the rock away and found a golden reed pipe.

When Redberry blew on the pipe, all the frogs and other creatures began to dance. The faster the tune, the faster they danced. "Aha!" cried Redberry. "Now I can deal with the dragon!"

When he came to the dragon's cave, he saw a girl dressed in red. Redberry blew on the pipe, and the dragon began to dance. The faster Redberry played, the faster the dragon danced. At last the dragon cried:

I'll send her home
If you leave me alone!

Redberry knew better than to believe a dragon. He kept on playing until they came to the sea. With a splash, the dragon fell in! Then the sister and brother returned home to their mother, who smiled with joy to see them.

> **Tip**
> From the title, you can draw the conclusion that the golden reed pipe Redberry finds is probably going to be important in the story.

> **Tip**
> How do you think Redberry plans to deal with the dragon? Read the rest of the story to confirm your prediction.

© Harcourt

1 **Because the story is a folktale, you know that it**

○ is based on real events.

○ uses an unreal event to teach something.

○ was made up and written down by the same person.

○ gives information about a topic.

2 **Here are some events from the story. Place the events in order from 1 to 4 by writing the numbers in the boxes next to each sentence.**

☐ Little Red's mother finds Redberry.

☐ Redberry moves the rock.

☐ Redberry sees the dragon.

☐ Little Red says her brother will rescue her.

> **Tip**
> Remember that you can look back at the story to help you recall details such as the order of events.

3 **When Redberry sees the frogs and other creatures dancing, he gets the idea**

○ to keep the animals as pets.

○ to entertain the dragon with his music.

○ to make his living playing the golden reed pipe.

○ to make the dragon dance and not let him stop.

4 **If the plot changed so that Redberry played an electric guitar instead of a pipe, how else would the story change?**

○ It would be set in a different time.

○ Little Red would not be rescued.

○ Redberry could be timid instead of brave.

○ There would not be a dragon in the story.

> **Tip**
> Try to imagine the story with the same characters, setting, and plot, but with an electric guitar instead of a pipe. What other part of the story no longer makes sense as a result of this change?

5 **Which statement expresses the moral of this folktale?**

○ A clever person can triumph over a fierce foe.

○ Look under boulders until you find what you need.

○ There is strength in numbers.

○ A dragon is powerless in its lair.

© Harcourt

Standards: 4-R2.8, 4-R2.1, 4-R1.10, 4-R2.1, 4-R2.4

Name _____

Directions
Read this retelling of a familiar fable. It has several mistakes that need correcting. Then answer Questions 6 through 8.

A Favor

¹A lion was fast asleep under a tree. ²A little mouse ran across the lion's face. ³The lion woke up and roared in anger. ⁴Grabbed the mouse in his huge paw. ⁵The mouse begged the lion to set him free and promised to return the favor some day. ⁶The mouse gnawed through the ropes and saved the lion.

---

6 **Which statement is not a complete sentence because it has no subject?**

- ◯ Statement 1
- ◯ Statement 2
- ◯ Statement 4
- ◯ Statement 6

Tip
Remember that the subject of a sentence tells who or what the sentence is about. Look for a statement that tells what a character does but does not tell who does it.

7 **What is the correct way to capitalize the title? If the title is written correctly, mark "Correct as is."**

- ◯ A favor
- ◯ a favor
- ◯ a Favor
- ◯ Correct as is

8 **Where would this sentence best fit in the paragraph?**

Then one day the lion got caught in a trap made of ropes.

- ◯ after Sentence 2
- ◯ after Sentence 3
- ◯ after Sentence 4
- ◯ after Sentence 5

Tip
Think about the sequence of events in the story and where this event makes sense in that sequence.

© Harcourt

Standards: 4-W1.5, 4-W1.5, 4-R2.1

GO ON ▷

Directions

Look at the underlined part of the sentence. Choose the answer that shows the correct punctuation for that part. If the underlined part is correct, mark "Correct as is."

9   <u>Frogs, worms, and, snakes</u> danced to the music.

   ○ Frogs worms and snakes
   ○ Frogs, worms, and snakes
   ○ Frogs worms, and snakes
   ○ Correct as is

Tip
Notice that the sentence has a compound subject. Think about the correct way to use commas in a compound subject.

10   Read the phrases. Look for an underlined word that contains a usage error. If the underlined words are used correctly, mark "All correct."

   ○ a <u>good</u> job
   ○ the <u>bestest</u> player
   ○ <u>most</u> amazing of all
   ○ All correct

11   Read the phrases. Choose the phrase containing an underlined word that is spelled wrong. If all the underlined words are spelled correctly, mark "All correct."

   ○ a <u>young</u> child
   ○ heading <u>north</u>
   ○ make a <u>promiss</u>
   ○ All correct

12   Write two sentences about music. Check your sentences for correct spelling, punctuation, and capitalization.

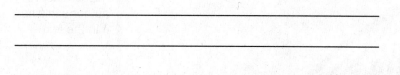

Standards: 4-W1.5, 4-W1.5, 4-W1.5, 4-W1.5

STOP

Name _____

Directions
Read the article below. Then answer Questions 1 through 5. You may look back at the article.

Iceland

Would you like to visit a land where you can see things that are both very hot and very cold? Iceland is a country that has both volcanoes and glaciers. That is why the country is called the "Land of Fire and Ice."

Iceland, about the same size as the state of Virginia, has more hot springs and volcanoes than any other country. In this small area, a volcano erupts about every five years! There are about 200 volcanoes in Iceland. It is one of the most active volcano areas in the world. In 1963, a volcano created the island of Surtsey. In four years, this island grew to about one square mile and rose to more than 560 feet.

Tip
Don't try to memorize facts about Iceland. You can look back at the passage later to locate facts you are asked about.

Much of Iceland is covered with the sparkling ice of glaciers. The third-largest glacier in the world is located in Iceland. Only the glaciers in Antarctica and Greenland are bigger.

Although Iceland lies just below the Arctic Circle and is partly covered by glaciers, the country is warmer than you might expect. The waters of the Gulf Stream in the Atlantic Ocean warm Iceland's climate. The average July temperature is a very comfortable 51° Fahrenheit. Of course, in winter it gets much colder.

Only about 250,000 people live in Iceland. This number is less than half of the population of Memphis, Tennessee. Most people who live in Iceland live in Reykjavik, the capital city. Iceland attracts visitors who like open spaces, nature, and outdoor activities such as hiking.

Tip
You probably don't recognize the proper noun *Reykjavik*, but notice that the author explains it in the text.

© Harcourt

1 Iceland is called the "Land of Fire and Ice" because

○ it has the world's third-largest glacier.

○ it has both volcanoes and glaciers.

○ it is warmed by the Gulf Stream.

○ it has 200 volcanoes.

Tip

Reread the beginning of the article, if necessary, to recall the author's explanation of what the title means.

2 Based on information in the passage, you can conclude that a glacier is

○ a large mass of ice.

○ a kind of volcano.

○ an island.

○ a hot spring.

3 Which of the following statements is an opinion?

○ There are about 200 volcanoes in Iceland.

○ Iceland is about the same size as Virginia.

○ The July temperature of 51° Fahrenheit is very comfortable.

○ The population of Iceland is about half the population of Memphis, Tennessee.

Tip

Remember that an opinion tells what someone thinks or feels about something. The statement cannot be proved.

4 Who would probably enjoy visiting Iceland?

○ someone who likes peaceful places and unspoiled nature

○ someone who likes warm weather and sandy beaches

○ someone who enjoys visiting art museums and theaters

○ someone who likes to shop and travel from city to city by train

5 Write a sentence or two to summarize the second paragraph in this article.

_____

_____

_____

Tip

Think about what should and should not be included in a summary. Your sentence should tell only the most important idea or ideas.

© Harcourt

Standards: 4-R1.10, 4-R1.10, 4-R1.13, 4-R1.10, 4-R1.9

Name _____

*D*irections

Read this paragraph from a report a student wrote about a bird called the kiwi. It has several mistakes that need correcting. Then answer Questions 6 through 8.

An Unusual Bird

¹ The furry brown kiwi does not look much like a bird. ² It has whiskers like a cat, and its feathers looks like a mouse's fur coat. ³ Rabbits and other animals also have whiskers. ⁴ The kiwi cannot fly. ⁵ It can walk almost silently on its soft feet. ⁶ It lives in the mountain forests of New Zealand.

---

6 Which sentence does <u>not</u> belong in this paragraph?

  ○ Sentence 2
  ○ Sentence 3
  ○ Sentence 4
  ○ Sentence 6

Tip
Think about the topic of the paragraph. The sentence that does not belong is the one that does not tell about that topic.

7 How can the error in Sentence 2 be corrected?

  ○ by changing *has* to *have*
  ○ by changing *its* to *it's*
  ○ by changing *looks* to *look*
  ○ by changing *mouse's* to *mouses'*

8 Choose the <u>best</u> way to combine Sentences 4 and 5.

  ○ The kiwi cannot fly it can walk almost silently on its soft feet.
  ○ The kiwi cannot fly, it can walk almost silently on its soft feet.
  ○ The kiwi cannot fly and it can walk almost silently on its soft feet.
  ○ The kiwi cannot fly, but it can walk almost silently on its soft feet.

Tip
Look carefully to see whether answer choices are run-on sentences or comma splices. Choose the compound sentence that is written and punctuated correctly.

*D*irections

Look at the underlined part of the sentence. Choose the answer that shows the correct punctuation for that part. If the underlined part is correct, mark "Correct as is."

9 The mother duck swam <u>away and</u> the ducklings followed her.

- ○ away, and
- ○ away. and
- ○ away and,
- ○ Correct as is

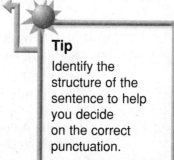

Tip
Identify the structure of the sentence to help you decide on the correct punctuation.

10 Read the sentence. Choose the answer that shows which word in the sentence should be capitalized. If the capitalization is correct, mark "Correct as is."

The city of oslo is the capital of Norway.

- ○ city
- ○ oslo
- ○ capital
- ○ Correct as is

11 Choose the word that is spelled correctly and completes the sentence.

The loud thunder _____ the horses.
- ○ scared
- ○ scaired
- ○ scairred
- ○ scard

12 Write a compound sentence about a place you would like to visit. After you write the sentence, check to see that you have capitalized and punctuated correctly.

Tip
Remember to use a comma and a conjunction to join the two parts of your sentence.

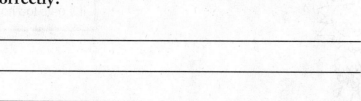

_____

_____

_____

_____

Standards: 4-W1.5, 4-W1.5, 4-W1.5, 4-W1.5

STOP

Directions
Read the poem below. Then answer Questions 1 through 5. You may look back at the poem.

How Hot Can It Be?

The thermometer said seventy-two.
That's not too hot at all.
"Seventy-two?" my mother said.
"That's only in the hall."

"It's much hotter," my mother said,
"outside in the sun.
I was out there with the neighbors,
and it's melting everyone!"

It must be very hot indeed
to make our neighbors melt!
Did they drip like candles made of wax?
I wonder how that felt.

How very hot does it have to be
to cause us to perspire,
and how much hotter yet
to make us feel like we're on fire?

Maybe it's ninety in the sun,
maybe a hundred and three.
I'm going out to play right now.
How hot can it be?

If I get too hot and start to melt,
I'll play beneath a tree,
but numbers on a thermometer
can't tell me how hot to be!

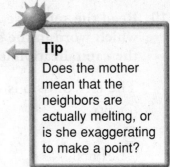

Tip
Does the mother mean that the neighbors are actually melting, or is she exaggerating to make a point?

Tip
Think about why the narrator of the poem might decide to play beneath a tree if it gets too hot.

© Harcourt

1 What does the mother mean when she says that the neighbors are "melting"?

   ◯ They have all gone inside.

   ◯ They are feeling very warm.

   ◯ They are burning candles.

   ◯ They are eating ice cream.

Tip
Look back at the poem to find the comparison. The word *like* is a clue that two things are being compared.

2 The narrator includes a simile that compares the neighbors to

   ◯ candles.

   ◯ thermometers.

   ◯ the sun.

   ◯ trees.

3 Which of these is <u>not</u> an example of an effect caused by heat?

   ◯ Candles melt and drip.

   ◯ People perspire.

   ◯ The thermometer rises.

   ◯ The sun shines.

Tip
Ask yourself whether each answer choice is something that happens as a result of the heat.

4 Which of these is true about the way the poem is written?

   ◯ The first and third lines always rhyme.

   ◯ The second and fourth lines always rhyme.

   ◯ The first two lines and the second two lines rhyme.

   ◯ Some lines rhyme, but there is no pattern.

Tip
To answer this question, look back at the poem to find the words that rhyme and identify the pattern.

5 Do you think the narrator should go outside to play? Write two sentences in which you give your opinion and then support it.

_____

_____

_____

Directions

Rick wrote a letter to his friend. For Questions 6 through 8, choose the answer that has correct capitalization and punctuation.

(6) _____

(7) _____

The weather here has been very hot, but my friends and I find ways to have fun and stay cool. How is the weather where you live? What kinds of things have you been doing this summer?

(8) _____

Rick

6　○ May 19, 20—
　　○ May 19 20—
　　○ may 19, 20—
　　○ may 19 20—

7　○ dear Matt,
　　○ dear matt
　　○ Dear Matt
　　○ Dear Matt,

8　○ your Friend,
　　○ your friend
　　○ Your friend,
　　○ Your Friend

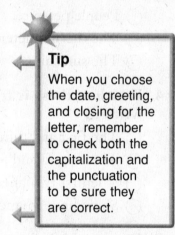

Tip

When you choose the date, greeting, and closing for the letter, remember to check both the capitalization and the punctuation to be sure they are correct.

© Harcourt

*D*irections

Look at the underlined part of the sentence. Choose the answer that shows the correct punctuation for that part. If the underlined part is correct, mark "Correct as is."

9 <u>Because it rained</u>, my bike got wet.
   ○ Because it rained
   ○ Because, it rained
   ○ Because it rained.
   ○ Correct as is

Tip
Notice that the sentence begins with a dependent clause.

10 Choose the word that correctly completes the sentence.

   Yesterday I _____ two new flowers in the garden.

   ○ see
   ○ seen
   ○ saw
   ○ sees

Tip
The word *yesterday* is a clue that the sentence tells about an action in the past.

11 Read the phrases. Choose the phrase containing an underlined word that is spelled wrong. If all the underlined words are spelled correctly, mark "All correct."
   ○ all the <u>children</u>
   ○ a <u>serprise</u> party
   ○ <u>birthday</u> cake
   ○ All correct

12 Write a sentence about something you like to do in the summer. Capitalize and punctuate correctly.

   _____

   _____

Standards: 4-W1.5, 4-W1.5, 4-W1.5, 4-W1.5

STOP

Directions
   Read the article below. Then answer Questions 1
through 6. You may look back at the article.

Manatees

Manatees are giant mammals that live in warm, shallow ocean
waters. They are harmless animals that feed on huge amounts
of sea grass, water lettuce, and other water plants. A full-
grown manatee can eat 100 to 150 pounds of plants a day!

Florida is home to the world's largest manatee population—
about 2,400 manatees. The population grows slowly because
female manatees usually give birth to only one infant every
two to five years. The low birth rate is one reason why the
manatee is in danger of disappearing forever.

Humans and their speedboats are the biggest problem for
manatees. Manatees are slow swimmers that swim close to the
water's surface. The propeller blades of a fast-moving
motorboat can strike a manatee and cause serious injury.

There are ways to help keep manatees safe. Because fast-
moving boats can't see the animals underwater until it is too
late, experts support slow-speed zones for boaters in areas
where manatees live. Another idea is to have boaters place
propeller guards on their boats.

One way to help manatees is to protect their homes by
keeping waters clean and limiting building on nearby land.
Protecting manatees in these ways may help to make sure
these interesting and gentle creatures will be around for a
long time.

Tip
If you are not
familiar with the
animal described in
this passage, read
on to learn more
about it.

Manatee Facts	
weight at birth	60–70 pounds
adult weight	1,500–1,800 pounds
food per day	100–150 pounds of plants
life span	60 years
average swimming speed	3–5 miles per hour
top swimming speed	20 miles per hour

Tip
Nonfiction texts
sometimes include
graphic aids, such
as charts and
maps, that show
information not
given in the text.

© Harcourt

1 **If humans don't take action to protect manatees,**

○ the manatees' food supply could run out.

○ boaters will need propeller guards.

○ manatees could disappear.

○ manatees will leave Florida for new homes in other places.

2 **You can find out the rate that manatees swim in miles per hour**

○ by skimming the article.

○ by looking at the chart.

○ by rereading the text.

○ by using both the text and the chart.

Tip
The text of the article mentions that manatees are slow swimmers, but does it give the swimming speed in miles per hour?

3 **What information about manatees is found in both the chart and the text?**

○ the amount of food eaten per day

○ the weight of a full-grown adult

○ what foods manatees eat

○ how many manatees there are in Florida

4 **All these phrases help you know that the author cares about manatees *except* the phrase —**

○ one way to help manatees

○ in danger of disappearing forever

○ interesting and gentle creatures

○ live in warm, shallow ocean waters

Tip
The word *except* tells you to look for the answer choice that does *not* show that the author cares about manatees.

5 **If you were not sure of the meaning of *infant*, which other word in the second paragraph could help you figure out its meaning?**

○ home

○ usually

○ birth

○ danger

6 **Write a sentence to tell the author's purpose for writing this article.**

_____

_____

_____

Directions

Look at the underlined part of the sentence. Choose the answer that shows the correct punctuation for that part. If the underlined part is correct, mark "Correct as is."

7 Scientists tell us that animals are sometimes <u>harmed, when</u> new structures are built.

○ harmed when

○ harmed when,

○ harmed," when

○ Correct as is

Tip
The word *when* in this sentence introduces a dependent clause. Think about where in the sentence the dependent clause is located. Does this part of the sentence need any form of punctuation?

8 Read the sentence. Then choose the answer in which the word *look* has the same meaning as it does in the sentence.

Kate went to school with a happy <u>look</u> on her face.

○ look at a picture

○ take a look

○ pears look ripe

○ a look of embarrassment

Tip
Notice that *look* is used as a noun in the sentence. Find the phrases in which *look* is used as a noun. Then decide which has the same meaning.

9 Choose the word that is spelled correctly and completes the sentence.

The crowd laughed when the whale _____.

○ spowted

○ spouted

○ spoughted

○ spooted

10 The word *preview* means

○ to look again

○ to look before

○ to look away

○ to look back

© Harcourt

Standards: 4-W1.5, 4-R3.4, 4-W1.5, 4-R3.3

Time to Write

***D**irections*

Think of important information about the environment that you have learned in school or from another source. Write a composition to inform others about these facts and ideas.

Writer's Checklist

Remember to:

❏ Introduce your topic in a clear and interesting way.

❏ State your main idea in a topic sentence.

❏ Present details that explain and support your main idea.

❏ Arrange your details in a logical order.

❏ Organize your composition into paragraphs.

❏ Include different types of sentences.

❏ Write complete sentences.

❏ Use correct punctuation, capitalization, and spelling.

Standards: 4-W1.1, 4-W1.2, 4-W1.3, 4-W1.5, 4-W1.6.1, 4-W2.1

STOP

Directions

Read the story below. Then answer Questions 1
through 5. You may look back at the story.

Only One Choice

Ben had dreamed all his life about doing something exciting.
Aunt Molly told Ben about her experience teaching river
rafting. She described how it felt to ride the currents and
coast the rapids. Then she asked Ben to go rafting with her.
Finally, he had a chance to make his dream come true!

On the big day, Aunt Molly was to pick up Ben at 10 A.M. As
Ben filled his backpack, he heard Mom yell, "Ben! Ben!
Hurry!" He raced downstairs and saw his little sister, Tori,
lying on the kitchen floor.

"I fell," Tori said. "My leg hurts, and my head feels funny."

"Call an ambulance, Ben," said Mom. "I'll sit with Tori."

Ben dialed 911. It was 9:15. Worried about Tori, he hoped
the ambulance would come right away. It arrived at 9:20, and
two workers gently placed Tori on a stretcher and put her
inside the vehicle.

"She hit her head," Mom told them.

"She'll probably be all right, but we should check it out
completely," said the driver. "You can climb in the back
with her."

Ben was about to jump into the ambulance when Mom
reminded him to stay behind so he wouldn't miss his rafting
trip. With all the excitement, he had forgotten about the trip!
Ben looked at his sister and saw tears in her eyes.

"I want Ben to go with me," Tori whispered to Mom.

Ben thought for a second. Then he said, "An ambulance ride
will be enough excitement for me today!"

Tip

The title often
gives a clue
about important
events in a story.
Read this story
to find out what
choice a character
has to make and
what he or she
decides to do.

Tip

As you read, make
predictions about
what might happen
next in the story.
What choice do
you think Ben will
make?

© Harcourt

1 Which picture shows an event that did <u>not</u> result from Tori's fall?

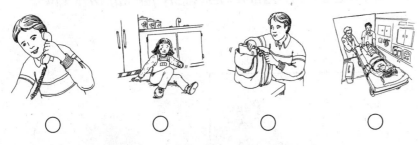

○   ○   ○   ○

Tip
Tori's fall was the cause of the events shown in three of the pictures. The correct choice shows the event that was *not* caused by the fall.

2 The problem Ben faces in this story is

○ figuring out how to get help for his sister.

○ deciding whether to go with Tori or to go on his trip.

○ getting his mother to let him go on the rafting trip.

○ being afraid that he will get hurt if he tries river rafting.

3 You can draw the conclusion that the title "Only One Choice" means

○ there is only one choice Ben can make and feel good about.

○ Ben has only one choice because his mother tells him what to do.

○ Ben's mother makes the right choice about calling an ambulance.

○ Ben makes the wrong choice about riding in the ambulance.

Tip
To draw a conclusion about the title, use details from the story and your own knowledge to figure out what the title means.

4 The words that <u>best</u> describe Ben are

○ selfish and uncaring.

○ honest and brave.

○ friendly and talkative.

○ caring and unselfish.

5 What do you think might happen next in this story?

○ Ben will blame Tori for making him miss the rafting trip.

○ Ben will decide he is afraid to go rafting.

○ Aunt Molly and Ben will plan another rafting trip.

○ Ben will lose interest in rafting and not think about it again.

Tip
Rereading the first paragraph to recall how Ben feels about rafting may help you eliminate some answer choices.

Standards: 4-R1.12, 4-R2.2, 4-R1.10, 4-R2.1, 4-R1.8

GO ON

© Harcourt

Directions

Look at this table of contents from a book called *Get Ready for Rafting!* Then answer Questions 6 through 8.

Contents		
Chapter		**Page**
1	Preparation	5
2	Equipment	23
3	Choosing a Location	35
4	Choosing a Guide	47
5	Safety Comes First!	71

6 **In which chapter would you look to find out what kind of shoes or footgear you would need for a rafting trip?**

○ Chapter 1
○ Chapter 2
○ Chapter 3
○ Chapter 4

Tip
Read the chapter titles. Think about the kind of information you might find in each chapter.

7 **Which would be a good question to construct before reading Chapter 3?**

○ What's the most fun part of rafting?
○ How old do you have to be to paddle on a rafting trip?
○ What kind of paddle is the best to use?
○ What makes a location good for rafting?

8 **A student is reading Chapter 4. Which of these topics is probably covered in that chapter?**

○ the best rivers for rafting trips
○ what clothes to pack for a rafting trip
○ how to tell if a rafting guide is well qualified
○ how to avoid accidents and injuries

Tip
Find the title of Chapter 4 in the table of contents. Pick the answer choice that is most likely to be covered in that chapter.

© Harcourt

Name _____

Directions

Read the sentence. Choose the answer that shows which words in the sentence should be capitalized. If the capitalization is correct, mark "Correct as is."

9 The coryville ambulance Corps is raising money to buy a new vehicle.

○ The coryville ambulance corps is raising money to buy a new vehicle.

○ The Coryville ambulance Corps is raising money to buy a new vehicle.

○ The Coryville Ambulance Corps is raising money to buy a new vehicle.

○ Correct as is

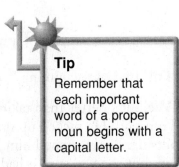

Tip
Remember that each important word of a proper noun begins with a capital letter.

10 Choose the word that correctly completes the sentence.

The girl said the backpack was _____.

○ hers
○ her's
○ she
○ she's

11 Read the phrases. Choose the phrase containing an underlined word that is spelled wrong. If all the underlined words are spelled correctly, mark "All correct."

○ silver and gold
○ bells jingle
○ in my pocket
○ All correct

12 Write a sentence that tells about something that you should not do at school.

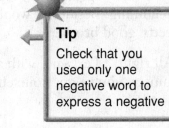

Tip
Check that you used only one negative word to express a negative

_____

_____

_____

*D*irections

Read the story below. Then answer Questions 1 through 6. You may look back at the story.

Trading Jobs

"I'm tired of vacuuming," Teri said.

"Well, it's better than taking out the garbage," her brother Tom said. He picked up the heavy, smelly bag and carried it outside. Teri watched him. Taking the garbage out was not fun, but she was sure it had to be better than vacuuming. She hated the high-pitched squeal, and she hated hauling around that monster of a machine.

"I have an idea," Teri said when Tom returned. "Why don't we switch jobs? Just for a week."

"Good idea," he answered.

By the end of the week, Teri decided that Tom was right. Garbage duty was terrible. The garbage cans always smelled. Also, the garbage had to be taken out every day! Vacuuming was just a once-a-week chore. "Let's switch back," Teri suggested.

At first, Tom didn't say anything. Finally, he said, "I like vacuuming. I pretend that I'm searching for treasure. I even like the sound the vacuum cleaner makes. It's a lot more fun than taking out the garbage. Couldn't we switch for good?"

Teri thought about it. Did she really hate garbage duty that much? At least she was able to go outside, and the job didn't take very long. It wasn't fun, but maybe it was better than vacuuming. Besides, it would make Tom happy, and he was a pretty good brother.

"All right," Teri said, with a laugh. "Tom the Treasure Hunter, you've got yourself a deal!"

Tip

When a story has dialogue in quotation marks, pay careful attention to be sure you know which character is speaking each time.

Tip

The details in this paragraph explain Teri's thoughts about garbage duty. Keep reading to find out what Tom thinks of vacuuming.

1 **Why does Teri call the vacuum cleaner a *monster of a machine*?**

   ○ The noise bothers her.

   ○ It is very large and very heavy.

   ○ It is unpleasant to use.

   ○ The vacuum cleaner is actually a monster.

2 **Write a sentence or two explaining why Teri and Tom decide to switch jobs.**

_____

_____

_____

Tip

If you don't recall what Teri means, scan the story to find the phrase *monster of a machine.* Then reread the sentence to figure out why Teri compares the machine to a monster.

3 **How does Teri compare garbage duty and vacuuming?**

   ○ Both have to be done every day.

   ○ Both smell bad.

   ○ Both are noisy.

   ○ Both are unpleasant jobs.

4 **Which of these is <u>not</u> a reason why Teri agrees to switch jobs in the end?**

   ○ She likes going outside.

   ○ She thinks garbage duty is fun.

   ○ Garbage duty doesn't take long.

   ○ She likes doing something nice for Tom.

Tip

Pay attention to the word *not* in the question. If necessary, reread the last part of the story to recall Teri's reasons for agreeing.

5 **Place the events from the story in order from 1 to 4 by writing the numbers in the boxes next to each sentence.**

☐ Teri decides she doesn't like garbage duty.

☐ Teri watches Tom take the garbage out.

☐ Teri tells Tom her idea to switch jobs.

☐ Tom tells Teri that he likes vacuuming.

6 **Which statement might be the lesson of this story?**

   ○ Two heads are better than one.

   ○ The best job is the one you enjoy.

   ○ Nobody should work all the time.

   ○ Work goes faster when you work together.

Tip

The theme of a story is like the lesson of a folktale. Think about what the characters did and what they learned at the end of the story. What did Teri learn?

© Harcourt

Standards: 4-R3.5, 4-R1.4, 4-R2.11, 4-R1.7, 4-R2.1, 4-R2.4

Directions

Read this paragraph from a report a student wrote about electricity. It has several mistakes that need correcting. Then answer Questions 7 through 9.

Electricity

[1] Electricity is the form of energy we use for light and often for heating and cooling. [2] Many of our most biggest machines and smallest appliances run on electricity. [3] Without electricity it would be difficult to live as comfortably as we do.

---

7 Which of these sentences would be the <u>best</u> topic sentence for the paragraph?

○ Some homes are heated by oil or gas.

○ Human beings get energy from the food we eat.

○ We can save energy by turning off lights when we leave a room.

○ We use many different kinds of energy, but electricity is the one we use most.

Tip
Try rereading the paragraph with each of the choices as the first sentence. Which sentence states the main idea that the rest of the sentences support?

8 What is the <u>best</u> way to rewrite Sentence 2?

○ Many of our most big machines and most small appliances run on electricity.

○ Many of our more big machines and smallest appliances run on electricity.

○ Many of our biggest machines and smallest appliances run on electricity.

○ Many of our most biggest machines and most smallest appliances run on electricity.

9 Which word in Sentence 3 should be followed by a comma?

○ electricity

○ it

○ would

○ comfortably

Tip
If you are not sure where the comma belongs, try eliminating incorrect answers. For example, commas are not used to separate subjects and verbs or to separate helping verbs and main verbs.

© Harcourt

Standards: 4-R1.9, 4-W1.5, 4-W1.5

Directions

Look at the underlined part of the sentence. Choose the answer that shows the correct punctuation for that part. If the underlined part is correct, mark "Correct as is."

10 Mr. Arnold <u>said, "Good</u> morning, class."

○ said Good

○ said "Good

○ said, Good

○ Correct as is

Tip
Notice that the sentence is quoting someone's exact words. How does an author punctuate the characters' dialogue in a story?

11 Choose the word that correctly completes the sentence.

_____ all the children finished their work?

○ Have

○ Has

○ Do

○ Does

12 Read the phrases. Choose the phrase containing an underlined word that is spelled wrong. If all the underlined words are spelled correctly, mark "All correct."

Tip
To figure out the correct spelling of a word with a suffix added, it is helpful to know the correct spelling of common suffixes.

○ a <u>worried</u> frown

○ as <u>darkness</u> fell

○ a <u>cheerfull</u> tune

○ All correct

STOP

Name _____

Directions
    Read the story below. Then answer Questions 1
through 6. You may look back at the story.

Melrose and Violet

Violet was the queen of the house. Visitors could spot her
black and gray stripes curled up on the leather couch, under
the blue chair, in the middle of the bed, or anywhere else she
chose to sleep at any time of day. When anyone reached
down to stroke the soft fur between her ears, she would purr
contentedly.

The only thing that could disturb Violet's peace of mind was
a visit from Melrose, who lived next door. Melrose was a big
orange cat. He always ate Violet's food as well as his own. He
even sat on her favorite sunny windowsill to watch birds.

Violet's owner, Barbara, was always baby-sitting this younger
cat for some reason. No reason, however, was good enough
for Violet.

One day, Violet decided she had had enough of Melrose.
When Barbara woke up that morning, she found Melrose in
his usual place on the windowsill. Violet was nowhere to be
found. Barbara remembered hearing angry hisses from Violet
when she fed the cats the night before. Had the noises been a
signal? Barbara looked all through the house, in every cabinet
and closet, and under every bed and chair.

Two days later, Barbara still had not found Violet. Melrose's
owner came by to take Melrose home and to thank Barbara
for taking care of him. Barbara had just gone back in her
house and closed the door when she heard a familiar sound. It
was Violet meowing at the door! Barbara opened the door
and scooped up Violet, who purred loudly. She was happy to
be home again and to be the queen of her own house once
more.

Tip

If you do not
recognize a long
word, use familiar
word parts and the
context to figure
out its meaning.

Tip

Notice that a new
character, Barbara,
is introduced in
this paragraph.
Unlike the other
characters,
Barbara is a
person, not a cat.

© Harcourt

1 **Violet is called the** *queen of the house* **because**

◯ she is fussy about her food.

◯ she gets her own way.

◯ she does not like Melrose.

◯ she lives in a castle.

2 **Melrose's visits disturb Violet because**

◯ Barbara pays more attention to Melrose than to Violet.

◯ Melrose makes angry hissing noises.

◯ Melrose eats her food and sits on her windowsill.

◯ she doesn't like Melrose's owner.

3 **Which picture best shows the meaning of the word contentedly?**

◯   ◯   ◯   ◯

4 **What conclusion can you draw about why Violet disappears?**

◯ She decides to live at Melrose's house.

◯ She gets lost and can't find her way home.

◯ She wants to show Barbara how she feels.

◯ She is looking for a new owner.

> **Tip**
> Authors do not always tell everything about a character. Use clues from the story and your own knowledge to draw a conclusion.

5 **Which sentence helps you predict that Violet will run away?**

◯ Violet was the queen of the house.

◯ Violet's owner was always baby-sitting this younger cat.

◯ One day, Violet decided she had had enough of Melrose.

◯ Two days later, Barbara had still not found Violet.

6 **Should Barbara continue to babysit Melrose in her house? Write a sentence or two telling what you think and why you think as you do.**

_____

_____

_____

© Harcourt

Standards: 4-R3.5, 4-R1.6, 4-R3.4, 4-R1.10, 4-R1.8, 4-R1.16

Name _____

Directions

Read this poster that a student made. Then answer
Questions 7 through 9.

CAT RESCUE CAR WASH
Saturday and Sunday
10 A.M. to 4 P.M.
8935 Hancock Road

Cars: $3.00   Vans and Trucks: $4.00

All money goes to support the work
of Cat Rescue. We need your support!

7   What is the main purpose of this poster?

○ to tell what Cat Rescue does

○ to tell where cats can be adopted

○ to inform people that the car wash costs more for
trucks and vans than for cars

○ to persuade people to go to the car wash

Tip

Read all of the
answer choices
before you decide.
The poster gives
certain information,
but giving that
information may
not be the *main*
purpose of the
poster.

8   The poster tells people that

○ the cash earned will be given to an organization
that saves cats.

○ getting a car washed will cost $4.00.

○ the car wash is on Monday and Tuesday.

○ the car wash begins at noon and ends at sunset.

9   The poster probably has pictures of cats because

○ cats are cute.

○ they will get people's attention.

○ they will make people want to get a cat.

○ cats will be given away at the car wash.

Tip

To answer this
question, think
about the purpose
of a poster or a
sign.

Standards: 4-R1.15, 4-R1.15, 4-R1.15

GO ON

*D*irections

Read the phrases. Look for an underlined word that contains a usage error. If the underlined words are used correctly, mark "All correct."

10 ○ <u>mail</u> a letter
   ○ <u>road</u> a bike
   ○ <u>right</u> turn
   ○ All correct

Tip
The underlined words are all homonyms. Think about whether each is spelled correctly or whether another word that sounds the same but is spelled differently should be used instead.

11 **Which sentence is written correctly?**
   ○ The sisters saw three blue eggs in a robins nest in their friends yard.
   ○ The sister's saw three blue egg's in a robin's nest in their friend's yard.
   ○ The sisters saw three blue egg's in a robins nest in their friend's yard.
   ○ The sisters saw three blue eggs in a robin's nest in their friend's yard.

12 **Read the phrases. Choose the phrase containing an underlined word that is spelled wrong. If all the underlined words are spelled correctly, mark "All correct."**
   ○ <u>sign</u> your name
   ○ hands and <u>nees</u>
   ○ giraffe's long <u>neck</u>
   ○ All correct

Tip
Watch out for words with silent letters, such as *cough* and *knife*.

Directions
Read the poem below. Then answer Questions 1 through 6. You may look back at the poem.

Hot and Cold

Have you ever been to the desert?

It's a land of heat and sand.

The sun shines hot in the sky.

The air is blazing and dry.

You're baked like a pie.

You might see a cactus nearby.

It's a land of heat and sand.

Have you ever been to the Arctic?

It's a cold and icy land.

Everywhere you see snow,

Above, around, and below.

You feel frozen from head to toe.

You shiver as frigid winds blow.

It's a cold and icy land.

Tip
Notice that the title of the poem contains words that are opposites. Read the poem to find out what the title means.

Tip
As you read the second verse of the poem, think about how the description of the Arctic differs from the description of the desert in the first verse.

© Harcourt

1 The word *blazing* means
○ cold
○ sandy
○ hot
○ dry

2 The poem compares a person in the desert to
○ the sun.
○ sand.
○ a cactus.
○ a pie.

> **Tip**
> Reread the verse of the poem that tells about the desert. Look for words such as *like* or *as* that signal a comparison.

3 Which of these is true about the way the poem is written?
○ All the lines rhyme.
○ None of the lines rhyme.
○ The second and last lines of each verse are the same.
○ Both verses have the same first and second lines.

4 Which statement is true about this poem?
○ It tells how two different places are alike.
○ It contrasts the desert and the Arctic.
○ It tells why the Arctic is better than the desert.
○ Its purpose is to persuade people to visit faraway places.

5 How might the phrase *baked like a pie* affect someone reading the poem?
○ It might make the reader want to visit the desert.
○ It might make the reader not want to visit the desert.
○ It might make the reader feel hungry.
○ It might make the reader dislike pie.

6 Write two adjectives from the poem that describe the desert and two that describe the Arctic.

desert   Arctic

_____   _____

_____   _____

> **Tip**
> Look back at the poem to find adjectives, words that describe nouns or pronouns.

© Harcourt

Standards: 4-R3.4, 4-R2.6, 4-R2.9, 4-R2.11, 4-R2.6, 4-R2.5

GO ON

Directions

Read this paragraph from a composition that a student wrote. Then answer Questions 7 and 8.

Two Extremes

[1] Would you want to live in either the Arctic or Antarctica? [2] It wouldn't be easy. [3] For one thing, it is difficult to adjust to the extremes of light and darkness. [4] The sun shines all night in the summer. [5] The sun doesn't come up at all in the winter.

---

7 **Which sentence would be the best closing sentence for the paragraph?**

○ Polar bears have white fur that helps them blend in with the snowy background.

○ Besides being dark, winter at both poles is extremely cold and windy.

○ Scientists who study the polar regions need the right equipment.

○ How would you like to live near the equator?

Tip
If you are not sure about an answer choice, reread the paragraph to see whether the sentence adds more information about the main idea.

8 **Choose the best way to combine Sentences 4 and 5.**

○ The sun shines all night in the summer but doesn't come up at all in the winter.

○ The sun shines all night in the summer, the sun doesn't come up at all in the winter.

○ The sun shines all night in the summer it doesn't come up at all in the winter.

○ The sun shines all night in the summer, or it doesn't come up at all in the winter.

9 **Which of these would be the best resource for finding maps of the Arctic region and Antarctica?**

○ a dictionary

○ a thesaurus

○ an almanac

○ an atlas

Tip
Read the question carefully. Notice that it asks specifically about maps.

© Harcourt

Standards: 4-W1.3, 4-W1.4, 4-RS2.1

*D*irections

Look at the underlined part of the sentence. Choose the answer that shows the correct capitalization and punctuation for that part. If the underlined part is correct, mark "Correct as is."

10 Carla lives in Charleston, <u>S,c,</u>

○ S;C.

○ sc.

○ SC.

○ Correct as is

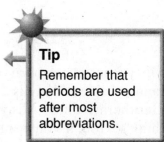

Tip
Remember that periods are used after most abbreviations.

11 Choose the word that correctly completes the sentence.

Both _____ caps blew right off their heads.

○ boys

○ boy's

○ boys'

○ boys's

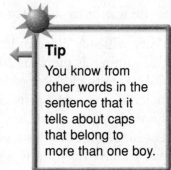

Tip
You know from other words in the sentence that it tells about caps that belong to more than one boy.

12 Choose the word that is spelled correctly and completes the sentence.

The high _____ peak was covered with snow.

○ mountain

○ mountan

○ mountin

○ mounten

STOP

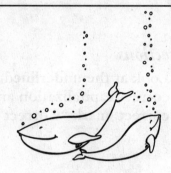

Directions
Read the article below. Then answer Questions 1 through 6. You may look back at the article.

Misty, the Blue Whale

Misty is just a newborn baby, but she is much bigger than human babies. Misty is 23 feet long and weighs about 2 tons! Her mother thinks Misty is just the right size, and you would think so, too, if you were a blue whale.

Like humans, whales are mammals and need air to breathe. Misty's mother pushed her to the surface of the water as soon as she was born so Misty could take her first breath of air.

Misty will stay close to her mother for the first year of her life, gaining as much as 200 pounds a day! She will also grow blubber, a thick layer of fat that helps keep whales warm in the cold ocean and provides them with food and energy. By the time Misty is finished growing, she may be as much as 95 feet long. Blue whales are the largest creatures of any kind ever to have lived on this planet.

For now, Misty's food is her mother's milk. As she gets older, she will eat huge amounts of fish and small sea creatures called krill. Krill range in length from less than $\frac{1}{2}$ inch to almost 3 inches. Misty's mother can eat more than 4,000 pounds of krill in one feeding.

Blue whales make loud moaning sounds that can be heard underwater more than 100 miles away. They are the loudest animals on Earth. The sound is louder than a jet. Scientists believe that whales use these sounds to keep in touch with each other as they swim beneath the surface of the world's oceans.

Misty will soon be big enough to join the other whales in her pod (group) in their yearly swim from the warm waters of the tropics to the cold waters of the Arctic and Antarctica. Blue whales like Misty travel long distances and are found in every ocean of the world. They are very fast swimmers and can swim as fast as 30 miles per hour.

Tip
The author does not tell you right away who or what Misty is. Read on to find out this information.

Tip
Trying to remember all the details in the article may confuse you. Read to understand the main idea. You can look back later to recall the details.

© Harcourt

1 **You can tell that this article is an informational narrative because it**

○ gives information about a topic.

○ tells about events that could be real.

○ is a story that presents information.

○ has animal characters.

2 **Misty is different from human babies because**

○ human babies breathe air.

○ Misty is much larger.

○ Misty is a mammal.

○ human babies require care.

3 **The article explains that krill are**

○ baby blue whales.

○ fish.

○ the sounds that blue whales make.

○ small sea creatures.

4 **You can use information from the article to draw the conclusion that blue whales**

○ prefer to be alone.

○ don't like other kinds of whales.

○ travel in groups.

○ spend most of their lives in one place.

5 **The author uses facts in this article to**

○ inform the reader about blue whales.

○ persuade the reader to help save blue whales.

○ entertain the reader with a humorous story.

○ warn the reader to stay away from blue whales.

6 **Write a sentence that summarizes the information given in the fifth paragraph.**

_____

_____

_____

_____

Tip

Try using each answer choice to complete the sentence. Keep in mind the key words *different from*. Which answer tells a way that Misty and human babies are different?

Tip

If you don't remember the answer to this question, scan the article for the word *krill*. Then reread that part of the article.

© Harcourt

Standards: 4-R2.8, 4-R2.11, 4-R1.6, 4-R1.10, 4-R2.10, 4-R1.9

*D*irections

Read this paragraph from a story that a student wrote. It has several mistakes that need correcting. Then answer Questions 7 through 9.

Keri's new pet

¹ Keri had always wanted a pet, but there was not enough room for a dog or cat in her family's small apartment. ² One day, though, her dad come home with a surprise—a golden hamster.

³ He told Keri that the golden hamster is easy to keep as a pet it is gentle and can live in a small space. ⁴ Keri would need to give her new pet food, water, a place to exercise, and clean bedding.

---

7 **Choose the correct way to write the title. If the title is written correctly, mark "Correct as is."**

○ Keri's New pet

○ Keri's new Pet

○ Keri's New Pet

○ Correct as is

8 **Which sentence contains two complete thoughts and should be written as two sentences?**

○ Sentence 1

○ Sentence 2

○ Sentence 3

○ Sentence 4

Tip
Look for a run-on sentence made up of two independent clauses.

9 **Which is the best way to rewrite Sentence 2?**

○ One day, though, her dad comes home with a surprise—a golden hamster.

○ One day, though, her dad came home with a surprise—a golden hamster.

○ One day, though, her dad is coming home with a surprise—a golden hamster.

○ One day, though, her dad has come home with a surprise—a golden hamster.

Tip
Check to be sure that the sentence you choose has the correct form of the verb and also the correct tense of the verb.

© Harcourt

Standards: 4-W1.5, 4-W1.5, 4-W1.5

Time to Write

Directions

Think of a change that students in your school could make that would make the school day more pleasant for everyone. Write a composition to persuade your fellow students to make this change. Include reasons and details to support your opinion.

Writer's Checklist

Remember to:

❏ State your opinion in the opening sentence.

❏ Introduce your opinion in a way that captures your reader's attention.

❏ Present your reasons and details in a logical order.

❏ Conclude by restating your opinion and calling for action.

❏ Organize your composition into paragraphs.

❏ Include different types of sentences.

❏ Write neatly and clearly.

❏ Edit your composition for correct grammar, capitalization, punctuation, and spelling.

Name _____

Directions

Read the directions below. Then answer Questions 1 through 6. You may look back at the directions.

How to Make a Model Volcano

Materials:

stiff cardboard
glue
newspaper
flour-and-water paste

small plastic cup
baking soda
vinegar

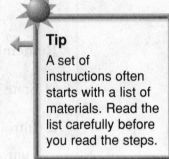

Tip
A set of instructions often starts with a list of materials. Read the list carefully before you read the steps.

Steps:

1. On the cardboard, make a circle of glue 6 inches wide. Crumple newspaper into small balls. Place the balls on the glue. Place glue on these balls and add more balls. Continue this process until you have a cone shape about 6 inches tall.

2. Tear more newspaper into strips. Dip the strips into the flour-and-water paste. Then place them over the cone to build a mountain. Cover the cone with several layers of wet newspaper strips.

3. With your finger, poke a large hole about 2 inches deep at the top of the mountain. Put a small plastic cup into the opening. Let the mountain dry for several days.

4. Now you are ready to make the volcano "erupt." Put 1 teaspoon of baking soda in the cup at the top of the volcano. Slowly pour 1 teaspoon of vinegar into the cup. Watch what happens!

Tip
Steps 1–3 tell how to construct your model volcano. Now read Step 4 to learn how to make the model volcano "erupt."

© Harcourt

1 **This passage is mostly about**
- ○ how volcanoes erupt.
- ○ how to make a cone shape from newspapers.
- ○ the materials you need to make a model volcano.
- ○ how to make a model volcano that erupts.

2 **Why does the volcano seem to erupt?**
- ○ The model volcano is very hot.
- ○ Flour and water dry quickly.
- ○ Vinegar and baking soda bubble and fizz when mixed.
- ○ The volcano is shaped like a cone.

Tip
The directions do not give the answer to this question. Draw a conclusion by putting your own knowledge together with information from the directions.

3 **The purpose of this article is to**
- ○ explain how to do something.
- ○ inform readers about types of model volcanoes.
- ○ persuade readers to visit a volcano.
- ○ tell an entertaining story.

4 **What information appears under the first subhead?**
- ○ things you need for this project
- ○ how to begin this project
- ○ what to do second in this project
- ○ what the result of the project is

5 **Where else might you find directions for making a model volcano?**
- ○ an encyclopedia
- ○ a science website for students
- ○ a dictionary
- ○ an atlas

6 **What would happen if you skipped Step 3?**

_____

_____

_____

Tip
Reread Step 1 and then Step 3. Would you be able to complete Step 3 without doing Step 2 first? Explain briefly the problem you would have.

© Harcourt

Standards: 4-R1.9, 4-R1.10, 4-R2.10, 4-R1.7, 4-RS2.1, 4-R1.12

Name _____

Directions

Read this paragraph from a report that a student wrote about how chairs were invented. It has several mistakes that need correcting. Then answer Questions 7 through 9.

Inventing Chairs

[1] Prehistoric people first sat on rocks. [2] Later, they begin to put wood on top of the rocks. [3] This arrangement became a type of seat. [4] After people invented tools. [5] They began to make chairs.

---

7 Which sentence is the <u>best</u> topic sentence for the paragraph?

○ People have been building with rocks since ancient times.

○ In some cultures, people squat or kneel.

○ Modern chairs come in a wide variety of styles.

○ Chairs have a long and interesting history.

Tip
The topic sentence should state the main idea of the paragraph.

8 Which is the <u>best</u> way to rewrite Sentence 2?

○ Later, they begins to put wood on top of the rocks.

○ Later, they begun to put wood on top of the rocks.

○ Later, they began to put wood on top of the rocks.

○ Later, they beginning to put wood on top of the rocks.

9 Which statement is a sentence fragment?

○ Statement 1

○ Statement 2

○ Statement 3

○ Statement 4

Tip
Look for a dependent clause that cannot stand alone and should be combined with other words to make a complete sentence.

Standards: 4-R1.9, 4-W1.5, 4-W1.5

GO ON

D*irections*

Read the phrases. Look for an underlined word that contains an error in grammar. If all the underlined words are used correctly, mark "All correct."

10 ○ for <u>us</u>
    ○ with <u>them</u>
    ○ told Mark and <u>I</u>
    ○ All correct

11 **Which word in the sentence should be capitalized?**

Our teacher asked us to read a magazine article about the planet mars.

    ○ teacher
    ○ magazine
    ○ planet
    ○ mars

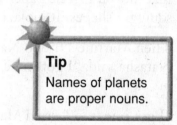

Tip
Names of planets are proper nouns.

12 **Choose the word that is spelled correctly and completes the sentence.**

That was a funny _____ !

    ○ story
    ○ storey
    ○ storie
    ○ storee

Standards: 4-W1.5, 4-W1.5, 4-W1.5

STOP

Directions

Read the story below. Then answer Questions 1 through 6. You may look back at the story.

A True Treasure

Martine peered at the paper she had found under her door that morning. The paper was torn and had dotted lines and squiggly shapes. It looked like part of a treasure map.

Then Martine's friend Natasha called. "Hey, Martine," Natasha said. "I got some weird piece of paper under my door."

"I got one, too!" cried Martine.

"I think it's some kind of map," Natasha said. "My piece has a big X on it!"

"Mine has Alameda Street marked off!" Martine said.

Their friend Valerie had a map, too. Hers had Third Avenue marked. Soon, the three friends met at the corner of Third Avenue and Alameda Street. Their pieces of paper fit together like a jigsaw puzzle. Starting at the corner where they were, the girls followed a dotted line on the map. The line wound around trees, down the sidewalk, and back to the street where they lived.

The three friends found themselves in front of Valerie's neighbors' house. Just then the front door of the house opened, and a girl came out carrying a plate of muffins.

"My name is Annika," she said. "I'm visiting my aunt for the summer. I wanted to meet some girls in town, and I wanted to make it fun. My aunt said you three might enjoy solving a puzzle together. So, we arranged this with your parents' help."

Martine laughed. "I thought we were going to find a treasure!"

"We did," Valerie said. "A new friend is a true treasure!"

Tip

Many of the sentences spoken by the characters end with exclamation points. What does this tell you about how the characters feel?

Tip

How do you think the story will end? Making predictions as you read will help you enjoy and remember the story.

© Harcourt

1 The three friends in the story speak in a way that shows they are

- ○ upset.
- ○ jealous.
- ○ bored.
- ○ excited.

2 You can tell this story is a mystery because

- ○ it teaches a lesson.
- ○ it tells about real people and real events.
- ○ the action centers on finding the answer to a question.
- ○ the characters do things that real people would not do.

3 The girls meet at the corner of Third Avenue and Alameda Street because

- ○ it is close to all their houses.
- ○ those streets are shown on the map.
- ○ that is where their school is.
- ○ Martine's mother tells them to meet there.

Tip

If you are not sure of the answer, go back and scan the story for the names of these streets.

4 The words that best describe Annika are

- ○ friendly and clever.
- ○ lonesome and sad.
- ○ curious and excited.
- ○ shy and unsure of herself.

Tip

If you are not sure which character is named Annika, look back at the story before you answer the question.

5 Here are some events from the story. Place the events in order from 1 to 4 by writing the numbers in the boxes next to each sentence.

- ☐ The three friends meet.
- ☐ Martine finds a paper.
- ☐ A girl comes out carrying muffins.
- ☐ The girls follow the dotted line.

6 Do you think the method Annika used is a good way to make new friends? Write a sentence or two giving your opinion and telling why you feel this way.

_____

_____

_____

Standards: 4-R2.5, 4-R2.8, 4-R1.12, 4-R2.1, 4-R2.1, 4-R1.16

Directions

Read this paragraph from a report that a student wrote about maps. It has several mistakes that need correcting. Then answer Questions 7 through 9.

Maps

¹ There are many different kinds of maps. ² Each kind is used for a particular purpose. ³ One kind of map helps drivers find out the names of roads and where the roads go. ⁴ Another kind of map show elevations, or how high or low the land is. ⁵ Mt. Everest is the highest mountain in the world. ⁶ Still other maps show the boundaries that people have decided upon to separate states or countries.

---

7 Which sentence does <u>not</u> belong in the paragraph?

○ Sentence 3
○ Sentence 4
○ Sentence 5
○ Sentence 6

Tip
The sentence that does not belong is the one that does not stay on the topic of the paragraph.

8 Choose the <u>best</u> way to combine Sentences 1 and 2.

○ There are many different kinds of maps each kind is used for a particular purpose.

○ There are many different kinds of maps, each kind is used for a particular purpose.

○ There are many different kinds of maps, and each kind is used for a particular purpose.

○ There are many different kinds of maps, each kind that is used for a particular purpose.

9 Which is the <u>best</u> way to rewrite Sentence 4?

○ Another kind of map shows elevations, or how high or low the land is.

○ Another kind of map's shows elevations, or how high or low the land is.

○ Another kind of map show elevations, or how high or low the land's are.

○ Another kind of map showing elevations, or how high or low the land is.

Tip
Read each answer choice carefully to be sure all the words are written correctly and that all verbs agree with their subjects.

© Harcourt

Standards: 4-W1.4, 4-W1.4, 4-W1.5

*D*irections

Look at the underlined part of the sentence. Choose the answer that shows the correct punctuation for that part. If the underlined part is correct, mark "Correct as is."

10 "Your backpack is under my <u>seat" Ling</u> said to Dorian.

○ seat, Ling

○ seat," Ling

○ seat." Ling

○ Correct as is

11 Which word <u>best</u> completes the analogy?

Read is to *book* as _____ is to *TV*.

○ *show*

○ *newspaper*

○ *picture*

○ *watch*

> **Tip**
> An analogy tells how different things are related. Think of how *read* is related to *book*. Then pick the answer choice that is related to *TV* in the same way.

12 Choose the word that is spelled correctly and completes the sentence.

Nina wrote a short _____.

○ paragraff

○ parragraf

○ parragraph

○ paragraph

STOP

Directions

Read the story below. Then answer Questions 1 through 6. You may look back at the story.

The Clever Carver

There was once a king who collected carved animals. He had many carvings, but he had no carved mouse. So he asked two famous artists to come to the castle.

"Each of you must carve a mouse so lifelike and real that my cat will think it is alive. I will put them down together to see which mouse the cat jumps on. The artist who carves that mouse will get a bag of gold," the king explained.

One week later the carvers reappeared. The first carver had made a wooden mouse that was a perfect copy of a real mouse. The other carver had cut his mouse from a strange material. It didn't look at all like a real mouse.

"What's this?" said the king. "The wooden mouse is wonderful, but the other one will never fool my cat."

"Bring in the cat," said the second carver, "and let her decide which mouse is better."

When the cat came in, she jumped on the second carver's odd-looking mouse. She didn't even look at the wooden one.

"You win," the surprised king told the second carver. "Now please tell me something. Why did the cat choose your work when it didn't even look like a real mouse?"

"I didn't carve my mouse from wood," the artist said. "I used dried fish."

The king laughed. "I'll have to give away two bags of gold," he said. "One goes to the artist who carved so well, and the other goes to the artist who carved so cleverly."

Tip

The first paragraph introduces the characters and sets the scene for the story.

Tip

As you read, make mental pictures of the characters and their actions. Doing so will help you understand and remember the events that take place in the story.

Tip

Predicting the outcome adds to your enjoyment and helps you understand the story. What answer do you think the second carver might give the king?

© Harcourt

GO ON

1 The word *reappeared* in this story means
- ○ came back again.
- ○ will not return.
- ○ acts in a silly way.
- ○ without trying.

Tip
Look for a familiar prefix, root word, and ending in the word *reappeared*. Combine the meanings of the word parts to figure out the meaning of the word.

2 The cat chooses the second mouse because
- ○ many cats like to eat fish.
- ○ cats don't like wood.
- ○ it looks more lifelike.
- ○ the second mouse is closer to him.

3 Why does the king give away two bags of gold?
- ○ He thinks the first carver did a better job.
- ○ He likes to give away gold.
- ○ He dislikes the second carver.
- ○ He thinks both carvers deserve a reward.

4 Which sentence <u>best</u> expresses the main idea of this story?
- ○ A cat chooses an odd-looking mouse.
- ○ A carver shows a king that cleverness can be as important as skill is.
- ○ Two artists carve two different kinds of mice.
- ○ A king who collects carved animals decides to hold a contest.

5 Write a sentence that tells how the king feels about the second carver at the end of the story.

_____

_____

_____

Tip
The question asks about the end of the story. Reread the ending and look for clues about how the king feels.

6 Tales like this one are told or written to
- ○ teach about events that really happened.
- ○ inform readers about life in other nations.
- ○ explain how to do something useful.
- ○ entertain and teach a lesson.

© Harcourt

Standards: 4-R3.3, 4-R1.10, 4-R1.10, 4-R1.9, 4-R2.1, 4-R2.10

GO ON

Directions

Choose the sentence that <u>best</u> develops the topic sentence.

7 *Cats are good pets for older people who live alone.*

○ *Some people prefer to live alone, while others do not.*

○ *Neighbors should check on older people from time to time.*

○ *Cats are good companions and don't require a lot of care.*

○ *Before you get a pet, you need to know how to take care of it.*

8 What is the <u>best</u> pattern to use for organizing a passage that begins with this topic sentence?

○ cause and effect

○ main idea and details

○ sequence

○ compare and contrast

Tip

Reread the topic sentence and the sentence you chose as your answer for Question 7. What pattern or text structure do you recognize?

9 The author probably wrote this topic sentence to

○ entertain readers with a story.

○ tell how to take care of a cat.

○ describe different kinds of cats.

○ persuade older people to get pet cats.

© Harcourt

*D*irections

Read the sentence. Then choose the answer in which the word *cover* has the same meaning as it does in the sentence.

10 The author's name is on the <u>cover</u> of the book.
- ◯ cover a great distance
- ◯ cover with a blanket
- ◯ under cover of darkness
- ◯ magazine cover

11 The word *rebuild* means
- ◯ build slowly
- ◯ build again
- ◯ build higher
- ◯ build faster

← **Tip**
Divide the word into its prefix and base word. Use the meaning of the prefix to help you determine the meaning of the whole word.

12 Read the phrases. Choose the phrase containing an underlined word that is spelled wrong. If all the underlined words are spelled correctly, mark "All correct."
- ◯ dark <u>sunglasses</u>
- ◯ <u>pertect</u> from harm
- ◯ close your <u>eyes</u>
- ◯ All correct

Standards: 4-R3.4, 4-R3.3, 4-W1.5

STOP

Directions

Read the story below. Then answer Questions 1 through 5. You may look back at the story.

Little Golden Hood

There was once a little girl who was called Little Golden Hood for the gold-colored cloak and hood she wore. One day she set off to take a cake to her grandmother.

Before long, she met a wolf. He asked in a friendly way where she was going. "I am taking a cake to Grandmother, who lives at the other side of the wood in the house near the windmill," Little Golden Hood told him.

The wolf took a shortcut through the wood to Grandmother's house. Grandmother was not at home, so the wolf let himself in, put on a nightcap, and climbed into bed.

A few minutes later, Little Golden Hood arrived. When she saw the wolf in the nightcap, she cried, "Grandmother, you look so much like Friend Wolf! What hairy arms you have!"

"All the better to hug you, my child," said the wolf.

"Grandmother, what great white teeth you have!"

"That's for crunching little children with!" The wolf opened his jaws wide. Little Golden Hood ducked, so all the wolf caught in his mouth was her hood. The wolf drew back, crying and shaking. The little golden hood had burned his tongue! You see, it was a special hood that kept its wearer safe from harm.

The wolf, howling and yowling, ran for the door. Just then, Grandmother returned carrying a sack. She spread the sack across the door, and the wolf jumped right into it. Then Grandmother tied up the sack and threw it in the river.

Little Golden Hood never stopped to talk to a wolf again. In fine weather, early in the morning, you can still see her in the fields with her pretty little hood, the color of the sun.

Tip

Does this story remind you of a familiar fairy tale? Read on to see how this story is like that one and how it is different.

Tip

As you read, ask yourself questions about the story. What might you see in the fields in fine weather early in the morning that is a golden color?

© Harcourt

1 Which picture shows the meaning of the word *wood* as it used in this story?

○   ○   ○   ○

2 Why does the wolf put on Grandmother's nightcap?

○ to keep his head warm

○ to play a trick on Grandmother

○ to make Little Golden Hood think he is Grandmother

○ so he can take a nap before Little Golden Hood arrives

3 Write a sentence telling what might have happened if Grandmother had gotten home before the wolf arrived.

_____

_____

_____

4 The wolf cries out because

○ he opens his jaws too wide.

○ he swallows red-hot coals.

○ the golden hood burns him.

○ hot tea burns his tongue.

5 You could <u>best</u> predict what the wolf in this story might say and do by

○ comparing the story to other folktales.

○ knowing what wolves are like in real life.

○ thinking about what you would do in the same situation.

○ thinking about how this story is different from other stories you know.

© Harcourt

Standards: 4-R3.4, 4-R1.10, 4-R1.10, 4-R1.12, 4-R1.8

GO ON

Name _____

Directions

Read these notes that a student took for a report about butterflies. Then answer Questions 6 through 8.

1. A butterfly's life begins when a female lays her eggs.
2. Next, a tiny caterpillar, or larva, hatches from the butterfly egg.
3. Some species of butterflies migrate more than 1,000 miles.
4. Finally, the cocoon splits apart, and the butterfly pulls itself out.

6 Which note does not belong in the same paragraph as the other three notes?

- ○ 1
- ○ 2
- ○ 3
- ○ 4

Tip
Three of the notes tell about events in a sequence. The other note tells about something that should be in a different paragraph.

7 The purpose of this report is to

- ○ retell a folktale about a butterfly.
- ○ describe the patterns of butterflies' wings.
- ○ inform readers about a butterfly's life cycle.
- ○ persuade readers to protect butterflies.

8 In a nonfiction book about butterflies, where would you look to find the meaning of an unfamiliar word?

- ○ glossary
- ○ index
- ○ table of contents
- ○ copyright page

© Harcourt

Directions

Choose the word or words that correctly complete the sentence.

9 The wolf's teeth were _____ than mine.

○ more bigger

○ bigger

○ biggest

○ most biggest

10 Look at the underlined part of the sentence. Choose
the answer that shows the correct punctuation for
that part. If the underlined part is correct, mark
"Correct as is."

What an exciting day this has <u>been?</u>

○ been!

○ been,

○ been

○ Correct as is

11 Choose the word that is spelled correctly and
completes the sentence.

These _____ are bright red.

○ berrys

○ berryies

○ berry's

○ berries

Tip

Think about the
spelling of the
singular noun
berry. Then recall
how the spelling
changes when the
noun is plural.

Standards: 4-W1.5, 4-W1.5, 4-W1.5

STOP

Directions

Read the story below. Then answer Questions 1 through 6.
You may look back at the story.

Aniz the Shepherd

A Folktale from China

A wealthy landlord hired a boy named Aniz to watch
his sheep. People liked Aniz and loved to hear him
play his flute. The landlord, however, was constantly
scolding Aniz. One day, the angry landlord smashed the flute
to pieces. Aniz wandered through the streets with tears
running down his face.

Soon he met an old man who made him a wonderful new
flute and taught him how to play it. Now Aniz played tunes
as sweet as the bees' sweetest honey. Even the animals of the
forest would gather around and listen.

One night the landlord dreamed about a white rabbit with a
black spot on its head. He told his sons that the one who
brought him that rabbit would inherit all his wealth.

The first son went to the forest and saw many animals
listening as Aniz played his flute. One was a white rabbit with
a black spot. When the first son grabbed the rabbit, Aniz
played louder. The rabbit kicked and wiggled and got free.
The second son tried the next day, but the same thing
happened. The third son had no better luck than his brothers.

Finally, the wealthy landlord went to the forest himself. Aniz
saw him and began to play his flute. The animals came and
made a circle around the landlord. There were rabbits, bears,
snakes, foxes, wolves, and other creatures.

"Please don't let them eat me!" the landlord begged. "I will
give you anything you want!"

"Very well. I will spare your life," said Aniz. "But from now
on, you must be kind to poor folk. When you get home, you
must give half of your riches to the poor villagers."

The landlord did as Aniz had said. Now the poor people of
the village could buy good food and warm clothing, and Aniz
was more popular than ever.

Tip
As you read,
contrast the way
the old man
treats Aniz with
the way the
wealthy landlord
treated him.

Tip
First, Aniz plays
louder. Then, the
rabbit gets free.
Think about how
the two events
might be related.

Tip
Are you surprised
by what Aniz wants
from the landlord?
What does his
request tell you
about the kind of
person he is?

© Harcourt

1 **This folktale is like other folktales because**

   ◯ it reflects the values of a culture.

   ◯ the main character solves a mystery.

   ◯ some of the events really happened.

   ◯ a moral is stated at the end of the story.

2 **The old man treats Aniz**

   ◯ harshly.

   ◯ obediently.

   ◯ suspiciously.

   ◯ kindly.

3 **What does the story mean when it says that Aniz "played tunes as sweet as the bees' sweetest honey"?**

   ◯ The new flute buzzed like a bee.

   ◯ Bees came to listen and got honey on the flute.

   ◯ The new flute had a beautiful sound.

   ◯ Aniz ate honey before he played the flute.

4 **The rabbit gets free because**

   ◯ he fights harder when Aniz plays louder.

   ◯ the first son decides to let him go.

   ◯ Aniz shouts at the first son.

   ◯ the other animals help him.

5 **What is the theme of this folktale?**

   ◯ White rabbits with black spots are good pets.

   ◯ It is important to be kind and generous.

   ◯ Playing the flute will make you popular.

   ◯ Give landlords anything they want.

6 **How does the landlord feel when the animals surround him? How can you tell?**

_____

_____

_____

Tip

Think about the characteristics of folktales. Pick the answer that is true both for this folktale and for others.

Tip

The cause and effect relationship between these events is not explained in the story. You can figure it out by eliminating answers that do not make sense.

© Harcourt

Standards: 4-R2.8, 4-R1.6, 4-R3.5, 4-R1.12, 4-R2.4, 4-R2.1

Directions

Read this paragraph that a student wrote for a report about rabbits and hares. It has several mistakes that need correcting. Then answer Questions 7 through 9.

Rabbits and Hares

[1] What is the difference between a rabbit and a hare. [2] One difference is that baby rabbits are born without fur, while baby hares are born with fur. [3] In general, hares are more larger than rabbits and have longer ears. [4] Most rabbits live in colonies with other rabbits most hares do not live in colonies.

---

7 Which sentence contains two complete thoughts and should be written as two sentences?

○ Sentence 1
○ Sentence 2
○ Sentence 3
○ Sentence 4

8 Sentence 1 should end with _____ instead of a period.

○ an exclamation point
○ a question mark
○ a comma
○ quotation marks

9 Which is the best way to rewrite Sentence 3?

○ In general, hares are larger than rabbits and have longer ears.

○ In general, hares are more larger than rabbits and have more longer ears.

○ In general, hares are largest than rabbits and have longest ears.

○ In general, hares are larger than rabbits and have more longer ears.

Tip

Two adjectives are used in the sentence to compare hares and rabbits. Pick the answer in which both adjectives that compare are used correctly.

© Harcourt

Time to Write

Directions

Think about someone you know or have heard about who used creativity to solve a problem. Write a story that tells how a character resolved a problem or conflict in a creative way.

Writer's Checklist

Remember to:

❑ Begin by introducing your characters and setting.

❑ Explain your main character's problem and how it began.

❑ Show how the main character used creativity to resolve the problem or conflict.

❑ Include interesting words and details.

❑ Include different types of sentences.

❑ Check to see that there are no run-on sentences or fragments.

❑ Begin sentences and names of people with capital letters.

❑ Use correct punctuation and spell each word correctly.

Standards: 4-W1.1, 4-W1.2, 4-W1.3, 4-W1.5, 4-W1.6.1, 4-W2.2

STOP

Directions
    Read the article below. Then answer Questions 1 through 5. You may look back at the article.

What's a Supermarket?

It takes many workers to keep a supermarket running smoothly. Goods flow constantly in and out of the market. As shoppers make their selections, the items must be replaced.

Supermarket Workers

Stock clerks put items on the shelves. They code the prices into the store computer and make sure the prices are visible on the shelves.

Meat workers prepare packages of meat and fish under sanitary conditions. They wrap each package in plastic to seal out air and germs. Then they place it on a scale. Finally, they attach a label that tells the kind of meat it is, the weight, and the price.

Tip
Notice how the information in each section is organized. Possible types of structures include main idea and details, cause and effect, sequence, and compare and contrast.

Finding Your Way Around

Shoppers have many ways to find the items they want. In large supermarkets, the aisles have signs that show the aisle number and the kinds of products found there. Some supermarkets have a directory on the shopping carts. Of course, shoppers can also ask a store worker.

A supermarket usually has a section for fruits and vegetables, a dairy department with refrigerated cases, and a frozen food department. In addition, many supermarkets sell greeting cards, magazines, and other items. Some supermarkets have ATM machines that make it easier for shoppers to get cash.

Checkout

After shoppers find what they need, they take the items to the checkout counter. First, the cashier looks for a bar code, a set of thin and thick black lines that can be read by the store computer. A laser scans the bar code, and the computer then sends price information to that cash register. Finally, the cashier tells the total, and a packer puts the items into bags. With the help of supermarket workers, the shopping is done!

Tip
This section is organized differently from the others. Look for signal words that give you a clue about how the text is structured.

© Harcourt

1 This article is an example of

○ realistic fiction.

○ a biography.

○ a persuasive essay.

○ expository nonfiction.

2 Which of these is <u>not</u> a way for shoppers to find the goods they need?

○ using a directory on a shopping cart

○ asking a store worker

○ using an ATM machine

○ looking for signs in each aisle

Tip
Pay attention to the key word *not*. If you are not sure which answer is correct, reread the appropriate section to see which choice is *not* mentioned there.

3 Which sentence expresses the main idea of the section "Finding Your Way Around"?

○ Some supermarkets have a directory on the shopping carts.

○ A supermarket usually has a section for fruits and vegetables, a dairy department with refrigerated cases, and a frozen food department.

○ Shoppers have many ways to find the items they want.

○ Some supermarkets have ATM machines that make it easier for shoppers to get cash.

Tip
All of the answer choices are sentences found in the section, but only one of them expresses the main idea of the section.

4 The "Checkout" section of the article is organized according to

○ main idea and details.

○ sequence.

○ cause and effect.

○ compare and contrast.

5 Write a sentence that tells the main idea of this article.

_____

_____

_____

© Harcourt

Standards: 4-R2.8, 4-R1.7, 4-R1.9, 4-R2.8, 4-R1.9

Directions

Read this paragraph that a student wrote about an oil spill. Then answer Questions 6 through 8.

The Alaskan Oil Spill

[1] In 1989, a supertanker was shipwrecked off the coast of Alaska. [2] It took three years, more than 11,000 people, and over two billion dollars to clean up most of that oil. [3] It was the worst oil spill in the history of North America.

---

6 Which of these sentences tells more about the main idea of the paragraph?

○ Oil is used to heat homes and to manufacture products such as gasoline.

○ People helped by cleaning the beaches and oil-soaked animals.

○ The capital of Alaska is Juneau.

○ Shipwrecks can be caused by storms, poor visibility, and human error.

7 What source did the student probably use to find this information?

○ yesterday's newspaper

○ the website of a local oil company

○ a newspaper article from 1989

○ an encyclopedia

8 What would be a good question to try to answer if you were going to write another paragraph on this topic?

○ How is oil made into gasoline?

○ What was the worst oil spill in South America?

○ What was the cause of this oil spill?

○ When was the first oil spill in North America?

Tip

Scan the article and think about the kind of information it contains. Then think about the kind of information that you might find in each of the resources named in the answer choices.

© Harcourt

*D*irections

Choose the word that correctly completes the sentence.

9   Our friends _____ come to help us.
   ○ has
   ○ have
   ○ is
   ○ are

10 Look at the underlined part of the sentence. Choose the answer that shows the correct punctuation for that part. If the underlined part is correct, mark "Correct as is."

   When his sister's bicycle chain <u>came off Jeff</u> wanted to help.

   ○ came off, Jeff
   ○ came off Jeff,
   ○ came off. Jeff
   ○ Correct as is

11 Choose the word that is spelled correctly and completes the sentence.

   Mike _____ forgot his wallet.

   ○ carelissly
   ○ cairlessly
   ○ carelessly
   ○ cairlisslie

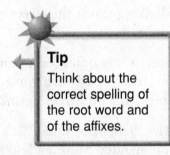

Tip
Think about the correct spelling of the root word and of the affixes.

12 Write a complete sentence about something you could not find in your supermarket. Edit your sentence for correct spelling and punctuation.

   _____

   _____

   _____

Directions

Read the story below. Then answer Questions 1 through 6. You may look back at the story.

Elm Street Is Renewed

Steven lives in Manchester, New Hampshire. The main street is called Elm Street. One day, Steven went looking for elm trees on Elm Street. When he didn't find any, he went to visit Mrs. Sanchez. She had lived on Elm Street for many years.

"The elm trees were gone long before you were born," Mrs. Sanchez told Steven. "A hurricane blew most of them down in 1938. Several years later Dutch elm disease made the rest of the trees sick."

"That's too bad," said Steven. "What were they like?"

"They were just beautiful," said Mrs. Sanchez. "Some were 100 feet high! They formed a canopy over the entire street. Walking down the street was like walking under an umbrella."

Steven was quiet for a minute. It seemed very sad that these beautiful trees were gone. "Do you think we'll ever have elm trees on Elm Street again?" he asked quietly.

Mrs. Sanchez smiled. "It's funny that you should ask that." She handed Steven a letter. "Go ahead, read it," she said.

The letter was from the city of Manchester. It described two new kinds of elm trees, the New Harmony and the Valley Forge, that could not get Dutch elm disease. Government scientists had worked for twenty years to develop these trees, and now they were ready to be planted. The city of Manchester wanted to know if Mrs. Sanchez wanted an elm tree in her yard again.

Steven handed Mrs. Sanchez back her letter. "Which kind will you plant?" he asked with a smile.

His neighbor laughed. "One of each, of course."

Tip
As you read, ask questions that will help you understand the story. For example, why aren't there any elm trees on Elm Street? Read on to find the answer.

Tip
As you read, make predictions about what may happen next.

Tip
Think about Steven's question. He doesn't ask whether Mrs. Sanchez will accept the offer. He asks what kind of tree she wants. Why is he so sure she wants an elm tree?

© Harcourt

1 The author's main purpose for writing this article was probably to
- ○ entertain readers with a pleasant story.
- ○ give information about the elm trees in Manchester.
- ○ persuade people to plant elm trees.
- ○ tell about events in the life of Mrs. Sanchez.

Tip
Eliminate answer choices that would not qualify as the author's main purpose until you are left with only one.

2 Here are some events from the story. Place the events in order from 1 to 4 by writing the numbers in the boxes next to each sentence.
- ☐ Steven reads Mrs. Sanchez's letter from the city.
- ☐ A hurricane blows down the elm trees.
- ☐ Steven goes looking for elm trees on Elm Street.
- ☐ Elm trees form a canopy on Elm Street.

3 Judging by the first paragraph, tell what you think Steven probably asked Mrs. Sanchez.

_____

_____

_____

4 Which statement is an opinion?
- ○ Elm trees can grow to be 100 feet tall.
- ○ Years ago Elm Street in Manchester was lined with elm trees.
- ○ Scientists developed new types of elm trees.
- ○ It was sad when Manchester's elm trees died.

5 In the eighth paragraph, Steven is sure about how Mrs. Sanchez will feel because
- ○ she has fond memories of the elm trees.
- ○ he has known her all his life.
- ○ she loves getting things for free.
- ○ he read what she wrote in her letter.

6 Replanting elm trees in Manchester is similar to
- ○ buying a new kind of rose bush.
- ○ bringing endangered animals back into the wild.
- ○ planting a large vegetable garden.
- ○ harvesting a crop of apples.

Tip
The question asks about returning elm trees to where they had been before. Which answer choice describes a similar activity?

© Harcourt

Standards: 4-R2.10, 4-R2.1, 4-R1.10, 4-R1.13, 4-R1.10, 4-R1.18

Directions

Read this paragraph from a report that a student wrote about fireworks. Then answer Questions 7 through 9.

Fireworks Facts

[1] Fireworks as we know them contain ingredients that make an explosion and make color. [2] The materials in fireworks that cause the explosion include powdered saltpeter, sulfur, and charcoal. [3] Other powdered materials are added to produce different colors. [4] Copper is used for blue. [5] Sodium is used for yellow. [6] Be careful around fireworks.

---

7 Choose the <u>best</u> way to combine Sentences 4 and 5.

○ Copper is used for blue, and sodium is used for yellow.

○ Copper is used for blue sodium is used for yellow.

○ Copper and sodium are used, they are used for blue and yellow.

○ Copper is used for blue, sodium being used for yellow.

8 The student probably wrote this paragraph to

○ encourage readers to see a fireworks display.

○ describe the beauty of a fireworks display.

○ tell a tall tale about fireworks.

○ give information about how fireworks are made.

9 Which of these is the <u>best</u> source for finding out what the word *sulfur* means?

○ an encyclopedia

○ a thesaurus

○ a dictionary

○ an atlas

Tip
Notice that the question asks about finding the meaning of a word, not about finding facts about sulfur.

© Harcourt

Name _____

*D*irections
Choose the word that correctly completes the sentence.

10 The trees _____ tall and beautiful before the wind knocked them down.

- ○ was
- ○ are
- ○ were
- ○ is

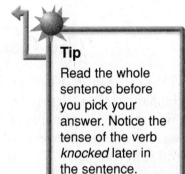

Tip
Read the whole sentence before you pick your answer. Notice the tense of the verb *knocked* later in the sentence.

11 Look at the underlined part of the sentence. Choose the answer that shows the correct capitalization for that part. If the underlined part is correct, mark "Correct as is."

The <u>Hernandez children</u> lived on Elm Street.

- ○ hernandez children
- ○ hernandez Children
- ○ Hernandez Children
- ○ Correct as is

12 Read the phrases. Choose the phrase containing an underlined word that is spelled wrong. If all the underlined words are spelled correctly, mark "All correct."

- ○ <u>write</u> a letter
- ○ sit <u>hear</u>
- ○ father and <u>son</u>
- ○ All correct

Tip
Homonyms, such as *right* and *write*, *hear* and *here*, and *son* and *sun*, sound the same but are spelled differently.

Standards: 4-W1.5, 4-W1.5, 4-W1.5

STOP

*D*irections

    Read the article below. Then answer Questions 1 through 5.
You may look back at the article.

The General Sherman

What is the largest living thing in the world? Is it an
elephant? Is it a whale? Actually, the world's largest living
thing is not an animal at all. It is a tree called the giant
sequoia, which grows in the mountains of California. You can
find it in the Sierra Nevada range.

The largest sequoia tree is called the General Sherman. It is
over 101 feet around at its base and almost 275 feet tall. It is
estimated to weigh more than 6,100 tons. The huge General
Sherman tree is also ancient. It is thought to be more than
2,200 years old.

Scientists believe there were many types of sequoia trees long
ago, most of which became extinct during the Ice Age. Only
three types are still found in the world today. Two of these—
the giant sequoia and coast redwood—are found only in
California. The other is the dawn redwood of southwestern
China.

European settlers in the United States first saw giant sequoia
trees around the time gold was discovered in California.
A hunter named Augustus T. Dowd was perhaps the first to
see the huge trees. He was in the woods near a town named
Murphy's Camp when he found a tree that was 24 feet in
diameter. The tree was cut down in 1853. It took five men
22 days to cut through it. You can still see the gigantic stump
of this tree in Calaveras Big Trees State Park.

Many people were upset that the huge trees were being cut
down. These people worked to make sure that some of the
giant sequoias would be protected. One of the first wilderness
preserves was set aside in 1864 to save these sequoias.

In 1890, Sequoia National Park, home of the General
Sherman tree, was established. Many giant sequoias today are
in parks, but some are still being cut down. Concerned people
are working to preserve these beautiful ancient trees for
future generations.

Tip
Use the numbers
to create a mental
picture of this huge
tree. Keep in mind
its great size as
you continue
reading.

© Harcourt

1 Why is the weight of the General Sherman tree given as an estimate?

○ It has stopped growing.

○ There is no way to determine its exact weight.

○ The scale broke when scientists tried to weigh it.

○ The author didn't want to bother looking up the information.

Tip
Use your own knowledge and common sense to figure out the answer to this question.

2 The information in the second paragraph of the article is organized according to

○ main idea and details.

○ sequence of events.

○ cause and effect.

○ comparison and contrast.

3 The information in the last three paragraphs of the passage, beginning with the words *European settlers* . . . is organized according to

○ main idea and details.

○ sequence of events.

○ cause and effect.

○ comparison and contrast.

4 Which of the following statements is an opinion?

○ There are three types of sequoias.

○ Sequoia National Park was established in 1890.

○ Sequoias grow in California.

○ Sequoias should be preserved.

5 Write a statement that tells what you think about the efforts to preserve the sequoias.

_____

_____

_____

Standards: 4-R1.10, 4-R1.7, 4-R1.7, 4-R1.13, 4-R1.16

Directions

Read this paragraph from a report that a student wrote about lilies. It has several mistakes that need correcting. Then answer Questions 6 through 8.

Florist Favorites

[1] The lily is a wonderful garden plant. [2] There are about 200 varieties. [3] Choosing among them is difficult. [4] Lilies are a great favorite with florists because of they're strong stems, rich colors, and long-lasting blooms. [5] In addition, many lilies produce delicious fragrances.

---

6 Which of these would be the <u>best</u> closing sentence for the paragraph?

- ○ Thanks to its beauty and variety, this special flower has earned its popularity.
- ○ If you love flowers, think about becoming a florist.
- ○ You may see other kinds of beautiful flowers growing wild in the woods or fields.
- ○ Whether you choose flowers or vegetables, gardening is a great hobby.

Tip
Some of the sentences use words from the paragraph but do not tell about the main idea. Remember that the last sentence of a paragraph sometimes restates the main idea.

7 Choose the <u>best</u> way to combine Sentences 2 and 3.

- ○ There are about 200 varieties, choosing among them is difficult.
- ○ However there are about 200 varieties, choosing among them is difficult.
- ○ There are about 200 varieties, so choosing among them is difficult.
- ○ There are about 200 varieties choosing among them is difficult.

8 The word *they're* in Sentence 4 should be replaced by _____.

- ○ their
- ○ there
- ○ it's
- ○ its

Tip
Reread Sentence 4 to find the error. Think of how to correct the error before you look at the answers. Then look to see if your answer is one of the choices.

© Harcourt

Standards: 4-R1.9, 4-W1.5, 4-W1.5

Directions

Look at the underlined part of the sentence. Choose the answer that shows the correct punctuation for that part. If the underlined part is correct, mark "Correct as is."

9 <u>Tomatoes and corn, grow</u> in the vegetable garden.
○ Tomatoes and corn grow
○ Tomatoes, and corn grow
○ Tomatoes and, corn grow
○ Correct as is

10 Choose the words that correctly complete the sentence.

When the wind _____, the tall trees _____.
○ blow, bend
○ blow, bends
○ blows, bend
○ blows, bends

Tip
Make sure that each verb agrees with its subject. When a noun subject ends with *s*, the verb that agrees with it usually does not end with *s*.

11 Choose the word that is spelled correctly and completes the sentence.

Let's work _____ to solve this problem.
○ togather
○ toogether
○ togethar
○ together

12 Write a sentence in the present tense about a tree or other plant that grows near your home. Be sure each verb agrees with its subject. Capitalize and punctuate correctly.

_____

_____

_____

Standards: 4-W1.5, 4-W1.5, 4-W1.5, 4-W1.5

STOP

Directions

Read the story below. Then answer Questions 1 through 5. You may look back at the story.

The After-School Club

Billy belonged to an after-school club. The purpose was to have fun while learning something new. Each week, a different member planned and ran the meeting. This week it was Billy's turn. He had everyone sit around a table. Then he dumped the contents of a large paper bag onto the table. All the members looked with interest at the variety of items in front of them.

"You have two minutes to memorize as many items as you can," Billy said. Everyone stared hard at the objects until Billy announced that time was up and returned the items to the bag. Then he asked how many items they remembered.

"I remember scissors, a spoon, a sugar cube, and a strainer," said Jan. "I memorized things that began with the same letter."

"I remember an apple, a cup, a glove, a map, a rope, and a watch," said Lottie. "I tried to put things in alphabetical order."

"I remember the scissors and the knife, the thread and the rope, and the cup and the glass," said Mark. "I tried to think of things that were alike in some way."

"I remember the glove, the rope, the apple, the strainer, and the scissors," said Rick. "I used the first letters of some of the things to make a word—grass."

"Each of you had a different trick that helped you remember what you saw," said Billy. "I'll bet there are even more memory tricks that we should find out about!"

The members all agreed that Billy's club meeting was one of the best they'd ever had. The following week would be Margie's turn. She had planned to tell jokes and riddles. Now she decided to do something that would better fit the purpose of the club.

Tip

You can tell from the first paragraph that this story is probably realistic fiction. You can also get an idea of what the story is about.

Tip

You don't have to keep track of the items that each student mentions. Instead, notice how each student remembers a different set of items.

Tip

The word *trick* has more than one meaning. How is it used here?

GO ON

1 The word *trick* is used in this story to mean

○ something done to fool someone.

○ an act meant to annoy or injure.

○ a special skill or way of doing something.

○ a practical joke.

2 When Rick uses the names of items to spell a word, he has to

○ alphabetize the names.

○ use the names of the largest items first.

○ figure out how the items are alike.

○ use the first letter of each item's name.

> **Tip**
> Reread the part of the story about Rick's memory trick and how it works. Find that part of the story by looking for the name *Rick*.

3 Margie changes her mind about what she will do at the next meeting because she

○ doesn't know enough jokes.

○ thinks Billy's idea is a good learning experience.

○ feels shy.

○ doesn't have enough time to get ready.

4 Write a sentence or two telling which memory trick you think is best and why.

_____

_____

_____

_____

5 Which statement best expresses the author's perspective?

○ You can learn and have fun at the same time.

○ All students should belong to clubs.

○ Having fun is more important than learning.

○ Clubs are not a good way for students to spend their time.

> **Tip**
> Think about the details the author includes in the story. Ask yourself what these details show about how the author feels.

Standards: 4-R3.4, 4-R1.7, 4-R1.10, 4-R1.16, 4-R2.10

Name _____

*D*irections

Read this paragraph that students wrote for a group project, and look at the graph they made. Then answer Questions 6 through 8.

Movie Attendance Survey

Our group did a survey to find out how often people go to the movies. We asked 50 of our friends and relatives. Here are the results of our survey.

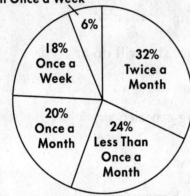

More Than Once a Week

6%

18% Once a Week

32% Twice a Month

20% Once a Month

24% Less Than Once a Month

6 According to the circle graph, how often do most people go to the movies?

○ once a week

○ once a month

○ twice a month

○ more than twice a week

Tip
The key phrase in this question is *according to the circle graph*. This tells you to use the graph to find the answer.

7 What information is found in the paragraph but <u>not</u> in the circle graph?

○ Few people go to the movies more than once a week.

○ Of those surveyed, 20% said they go to the movies once a month.

○ A total of 50 people were interviewed for the survey.

○ Fewer people go to the movies once a month than twice a month.

8 The circle graph shows you

○ how frequently people go to the movies.

○ what types of movies are most popular.

○ how many people go to movies and why they go.

○ why people of different ages like different movies.

Tip
Take another look at the graph. Does it tell anything about the types of movies people like or why they go to the movies?

Standards: 4-R1.15, 4-R1.15, 4-R1.15

Name _____

*D*irections

Choose the words that correctly complete the sentence.

9 We _____ good-bye when the ship _____.

○ wave, sailed
○ waved, sailed
○ waved, will sail
○ will wave, sailed

10 Which word <u>best</u> completes the analogy?

Hand is to *glove* as *foot* is to _____.

○ *walk*
○ *toe*
○ *fist*
○ *shoe*

> **Tip**
> An analogy tells how different things are related. Think of how *hand* is related to *glove*. Then pick the answer choice that is related to *foot* in the same way.

11 Choose the word that is spelled correctly and completes the sentence.

Take _____ time and don't rush.

○ you're
○ your
○ you'r
○ youre

12 Write two sentences about remembering things. After you finish, check to see that you have capitalized and punctuated correctly.

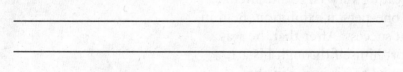

_____

_____

_____

Standards: 4-W1.5, 4-R3.6, 4-W1.5, 4-W1.5

STOP

Directions
Read the article below. Then answer Questions 1 through 5.
You may look back at the article.

Luis Jiménez—A Sculptor's Story

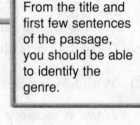
Sculptor Luis Jiménez was born in 1940 in El Paso, Texas.
At the age of six, he began helping in his father's neon sign
workshop. Luis learned many skills. By the time he was
sixteen years old, he could make glass, weld metal, and
work tin.

Young Luis learned about art in other ways, too.
He read books and visited museums. On visits
to Mexico, his family's homeland, he saw large
murals painted by famous artists such as José
Clemente Orozco. His experiences in Mexico
gave Luis pride in his heritage and influenced his
artwork.

In 1964, Luis Jiménez earned a degree in art at
the University of Texas. He has said that college
gave him a chance to see and study things he
would otherwise not have known about.

In his early years as an artist, Luis Jiménez found that some
people did not appreciate his favorite subject matter. He was
told that serious artists did not work with subjects such as
cowboys, Native Americans, and horses. To Luis, however,
these images were important and worthwhile.

From 1966 to 1972, Luis Jiménez lived and worked in New
York City. There he began creating very large and lifelike
fiberglass sculptures. His first one-person exhibition, held in
New York in 1969, was a great success. After that, he was
able for the first time to support himself through his art.
Eventually, Luis Jiménez returned to his home in the
Southwest. He now lives and works in a former schoolhouse
in New Mexico.

Luis Jiménez has received many awards and honors for his
work. His large public sculptures can be seen in cities all
over the United States. His most famous sculpture is called
Vaquero, which means "cowboy." Another of his sculptures,
a 32-foot-tall mustang, or wild horse, will be displayed at
Denver International Airport. Today, nobody tells him that
cowboys, Native Americans, and horses are not appropriate
subjects for serious art.

© Harcourt

1 **This article is an example of**

○ realistic fiction.

○ a biography.

○ historical fiction.

○ a folktale.

2 **Which of these words in the article means "having value"?**

○ appropriate

○ favorite

○ lifelike

○ worthwhile

3 **Which activity is not mentioned in the article as a way that Luis Jiménez learned about art?**

○ reading books

○ working in his father's shop

○ painting murals in school

○ visiting Mexico

Tip
Pay attention to the word *not*. Reread the first part of the article to recall how Luis Jiménez learned about art. The correct answer is the activity that is *not* mentioned.

4 **Luis Jiménez was told that if he continued to create art having to do with Western subjects, he would**

○ not be able to sell his paintings or sculptures.

○ have to go back to the Southwest.

○ never be considered a serious artist.

○ receive many awards and honors someday.

5 **Choose three important events from Luis Jiménez's life. List them in the order in which they happened.**

(1) _____

(2) _____

(3) _____

Tip
Look back at the article to recall the correct order of the events you have chosen. Use clues such as dates and time-order words to determine the sequence.

© Harcourt

Standards: 4-R2.8, 4-R3.4, 4-R1.7, 4-R1.6, 4-R1.4

*D*irections

Choose the words that correctly complete the sentence.

6 Rita _____ a long time before she _____ a name for her new kitten.

- ○ thinked, choosed
- ○ thinked, chose
- ○ thought, choosed
- ○ thought, chose

Tip

Think and *choose* are examples of irregular verbs. What do you know about the past tense of an irregular verb?

7 Look at the underlined part of the sentence. Choose the answer that shows the correct punctuation for that part. If the underlined part is correct, mark "Correct as is."

David has never skated but he wants to learn.

- ○ skated. but he
- ○ skated but, he
- ○ skated, but he
- ○ Correct as is

8 Choose the word that is spelled correctly and completes the sentence.

The car stopped at the stop _____.

- ○ sign
- ○ sine
- ○ sighn
- ○ sien

Tip

Remember that some letters are silent. If you don't hear the sound for a letter that you see in a word, the word may still be spelled correctly.

9 Write a sentence about a sculpture or painting you have seen. After you finish, check to see that you have used correct grammar, capitalization, punctuation, and spelling.

_____

_____

_____

© Harcourt

Standards: 4-W1.5, 4-W1.5, 4-W1.5, 4-W1.5

Time to Write

Directions

Write one or more paragraphs to persuade others to visit a particular place in your community. Include reasons and details to support your ideas.

Plan your writing on a sheet of blank paper. Then write the composition on a separate sheet of paper.

Writer's Checklist

Remember to:

❏ State your opinion clearly.

❏ Use specific reasons and details to support your opinion.

❏ Be sure all of your sentences relate to your topic.

❏ Include a variety of sentence types.

❏ Use interesting words and phrases.

❏ Use correct grammar, punctuation, capitalization, and spelling.

❏ Use complete sentences.

❏ Write clearly and neatly.

Standards: 4-W1.1, 4-W1.2, 4-W1.3, 4-W1.4, 4-W1.5, 4-W1.6.1, 4-W2.1

STOP

***D**irections*

Read the article below. Then answer Questions 1 through 5. You may look back at the article.

The Lewis and Clark Expedition

In his first term in office, President Thomas Jefferson nearly doubled the size of the United States in one move. He did this by buying a huge territory from the French government in what came to be called the Louisiana Purchase. The territory stretched west from the Mississippi River to the Rocky Mountains.

President Jefferson asked Meriwether Lewis to head an expedition to explore the new land. Lewis asked Lieutenant William Clark to lead it with him. Their plan was to travel by boat up the Missouri River, walk to the Columbia River, and then travel by boat again to the Pacific Ocean.

The expedition began in May of 1804. In October, they reached a Mandan Indian village. There they hired Toussaint Charbonneau, a French interpreter. His Native American wife, Sacagawea, proved to be a better guide and interpreter than her husband. She helped the explorers find their way through the unfamiliar territory.

After a year, Lewis and Clark expected to find the Columbia River. Instead, they saw only mountains stretching before them. Just when finding the river seemed hopeless, the explorers met a group of Shoshoni Indians. Sacagawea recognized one of the chiefs as her brother. He sold the group many horses and found them a new guide. In 1805, they reached the Pacific Ocean.

After more than two years, the explorers returned to their starting point in St. Louis, Missouri. The Lewis and Clark Expedition was one of the most important journeys ever taken in this country. Lewis and Clark helped map new territory and provided information about the people, plants, and animals that lived there.

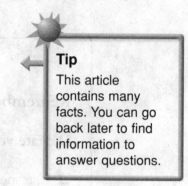

Tip

This article contains many facts. You can go back later to find information to answer questions.

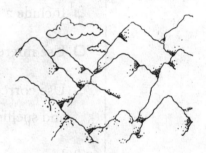

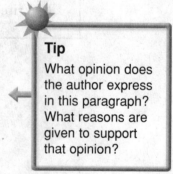

Tip

What opinion does the author express in this paragraph? What reasons are given to support that opinion?

© Harcourt

Lewis and Clark Expedition Time Line

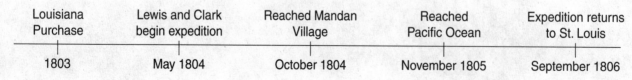

Louisiana Purchase	Lewis and Clark begin expedition	Reached Mandan Village	Reached Pacific Ocean	Expedition returns to St. Louis
1803	May 1804	October 1804	November 1805	September 1806

1 **This article is expository nonfiction because it**
○ presents and explains information.
○ tells a story.
○ combines elements of fiction and nonfiction.
○ is set in the past.

2 **Which of these sentences expresses an opinion?**
○ The territory stretched west from the Mississippi River to the Rocky Mountains.
○ They saw only mountains stretching before them.
○ The Lewis and Clark Expedition was one of the most important journeys ever taken in this country.
○ More than two years after they began their journey, the explorers returned to their starting point in St. Louis, Missouri.

> **Tip**
> Remember that an opinion tells what someone feels or believes. The statement cannot be proved.

3 **Which of these facts supports the opinion you identified in Question 2?**
○ The land was bought from the French government.
○ The expedition began in May 1804.
○ Lewis asked Clark to lead the expedition with him.
○ Lewis and Clark helped make maps of the new territory.

4 **What information can you learn from the time line that is not given in the article?**
○ The expedition began in 1804.
○ The journey took more than two years.
○ The Louisiana Purchase took place in 1803.
○ The expedition began and ended in St. Louis.

> **Tip**
> Pay attention to the word *not*. It tells you that the correct answer is the information found only on the time line, not in the article.

5 **Write one or two sentences to summarize this article.**

_____

_____

_____

© Harcourt

Directions

Read this paragraph from a report a student wrote about a surprising discovery. It has several mistakes that need correcting. Then answer Questions 6 through 8.

---

[1] In 1991, two hikers on a mountain trail in northern Italy spotted something nearby. [2] There in the melting ice. [3] Was a mysterious form. [4] It was a hunter who has died more than 5,000 years ago. [5] Scientists hurried to the site to remove the remains and begin studying this important find.

---

6 What should be done with the groups of words numbered 2 and 3?

○ They should be switched around.

○ They should be combined to make a sentence.

○ They should be moved to the end of the paragraph.

○ They should be eliminated.

Tip
A fragment is an incomplete sentence. Sometimes fragments can be corrected by combining them with other phrases or with sentences.

7 Which is the **best** way to rewrite Sentence 4?

○ It was a hunter who had died more than 5,000 years ago.

○ It is a hunter who has died more than 5,000 years ago.

○ It has been a hunter who has died more than 5,000 years ago.

○ It had been a hunter who have died more than 5,000 years ago

8 The word *site* in Sentence 5 means

○ to rest on a seat.

○ ability to see.

○ place.

○ a large town.

Tip
If you don't know this word, reread the sentence and use the context to figure out its meaning.

© Harcourt

Directions

Look at the underlined part of the sentence. Choose the answer that shows the correct wording for that part. If the underlined part is correct, mark "Correct as is."

9 He didn't do <u>none</u> of the work.

○ do none

○ did not do none

○ didn't do any

○ Correct as is

> Remember that it is an error to use two negatives in a sentence.

10 Read the phrases. Look for an underlined word that contains a usage error. If all the underlined words are used correctly, mark "All correct."

○ Sam's and <u>our's</u>

○ <u>we're</u> ready

○ <u>shouldn't</u> take long

○ All correct

> **Tip**
> Decide whether each underlined word is a contraction or a possessive pronoun.

11 Choose the word that is spelled correctly and completes the sentence.

He _____ go there often.

○ doesnt

○ does'nt

○ doesnt'

○ doesn't

12 Write a sentence about exploring or explorers. After you finish, check your spelling, capitalization, and punctuation.

_____

_____

_____

Standards: 4-W1.5, 4-W1.5, 4-W1.5, 4-W1.5

Lesson 26   111   **STOP**

Directions

Read the story below. Then answer Questions 1
through 5. You may look back at the story.

Walking the Wilderness Road

Jesse smelled the strong scent and hoped there was time to warn
his younger brother. He turned and ran, almost knocking
Bobby over. Both of them yelled as the skunk appeared. The
boys sprinted down the hill, the wind whipping at their faces.
They were only feet in front of the foul odor at their heels.

"Jess, this isn't fun anymore!" Bobby wailed.

By the time the boys reached the tent, tears flowed down
Bobby's cheeks.

"What is going on here?" their mother asked.

"We were playing in the woods, and Bobby scared a skunk,"
Jesse replied.

Helen Dantzler softly rubbed her youngest son's head. "The
skunks will stay far away from us on our journey. We'll be
traveling in a big group with <u>scores</u> of other folks. Now, finish
packing your bundles."

Two weeks later, the Dantzlers marched through the
Appalachian Mountains on the Wilderness Road alongside
four other families. Their possessions were strapped onto
packhorses. Jesse and Bobby struggled to keep the animals
on the rocky path.

It was 1784, and the Dantzlers sought new lands on the
Kentucky frontier. The road they traveled had been cleared
only nine years before by a group led by the famous pioneer
Daniel Boone. Since then, hundreds of families had followed the
boulder-strewn trail through the mountains.

"Dad, did Daniel Boone have this much trouble?" Jesse asked.

"You can ask him yourself, son." Joseph Dantzler replied. "There's
word that he's settled in his old fort along the Kentucky River."

Two days later, Jesse Dantzler got his answer from Daniel Boone.

"You probably had better luck than I did with packhorses,
young fella!" the famous frontiersman laughed. Jesse smiled at
his dad.

Another frontier family had begun life in Kentucky.

> **Tip**
>
> You may not know
> this meaning of
> the word *scores*,
> but you can use
> word relationships
> to figure out its
> meaning.

© Harcourt

GO ON

1 You can guess that this story is historical fiction because

○ it is told in the third person.

○ the characters do things that real people would not do.

○ it is set in a real time and place in the past.

○ the reader must use clues to solve the mystery.

2 You can figure out the meaning of the word *scores* in the story from

○ the word *journey* in the sentence before.

○ the words *big group* in the same sentence.

○ the words *finish packing* in the next sentence.

○ the word *packhorses* in the next paragraph.

3 The author probably mentioned the skunk to show

○ dangers in the wilderness.

○ a favorite game of pioneer children.

○ the way families behaved in the wilderness.

○ an imaginary situation that could never really happen.

4 Why did the author include facts about how the Wilderness Road was cleared?

○ to make the reader feel the emotions the Dantzlers felt

○ to make the story seem more realistic

○ to persuade the reader to move to the wilderness

○ to tell how to establish a trail

5 Write one or two sentences summarizing the first paragraph.

_____

_____

_____

© Harcourt

Standards: 4-R2.8, 4-R3.4, 4-R2.10, 4-R2.10, 4-R1.4

Directions

Read this paragraph from a report a student wrote about settlers on the Great Plains. It has several mistakes that need correcting. Then answer Questions 6 through 8.

Pioneers

¹ Settlers who came to make their homes on the Great Plains found rich grasslands but no trees. ² They had no wood for building homes, so many of them building houses of sod. ³ Houses in different parts of the world are built from a variety of materials. ⁴ Sod is soil held together by the tangled roots of grass and weeds. ⁵ The settlers cut the sod into blocks and piled them in rows to build walls.

---

6 Which sentence does not belong in the paragraph?

○ Sentence 2

○ Sentence 3

○ Sentence 4

○ Sentence 5

Tip
First identify the topic or main idea of the paragraph. The sentence that does not belong is the one that does not tell about that topic.

7 Which is the best way to rewrite Sentence 2?

○ They had no wood for building homes, so many of them build houses of sod.

○ They had no wood for building homes, so many of them are building houses of sod.

○ They had no wood for building homes, so many of them built houses of sod.

○ They had no wood for building homes, so many of them has built houses of sod.

8 Which of these resources would be most helpful in gathering information for this report?

○ an on-line encyclopedia article about the Great Plains

○ a website that shows homes for sale

○ a map of the United States that shows the Great Plains

○ a chapter about soil in a science textbook

Tip
Think about the kinds of information you might find in each of the resources. Which one is most likely to give the kinds of facts used in the paragraph?

© Harcourt

*D*irections

Choose the word that correctly completes the sentence.

9 The women walked _____ down the path.

- ○ swift
- ○ swifter
- ○ swiftly
- ○ swiftness

10 Read the phrases. Choose the phrase containing an underlined word that is spelled wrong. If all the underlined words are spelled correctly, mark "All correct."

- ○ a boat's white <u>sail</u>
- ○ pick a purple <u>flower</u>
- ○ <u>sore</u> into the sky
- ○ All correct

11 Write a sentence about an adventure you have had. When you have finished, check to see that you have capitalized and punctuated the sentence correctly.

_____

_____

_____

Tip
The word that correctly completes the sentence describes the verb *walked.* Which of the answer choices is an adverb?

Tip
Homonyms like *sail* and *sale,* *flower* and *flour,* or *sore* and *soar* are easy to confuse.

© Harcourt

Directions

Read the story below. Then answer Questions 1 through 5. You may look back at the story.

A Famous Beaver

The mountains of West Virginia were so rough and rocky that only the mightiest pioneers could settle there. Even among these pioneers, the Beaver family was unusual. Paw and Maw Beaver lived in a log cabin on top of a hill with the three little Beavers, who were named Betsey, Tony, and Molly.

Betsey and Molly were growing up big and healthy, but Tony grew so extra large that Maw sent him to strike out on his own. Tony set out, stepping from mountaintop to mountaintop, until he came to Turtle Cove. There he met Big Bill Simpson, who invited him to join a woodchopping contest.

Tony had chopped down trees for Paw, so he told Big Bill he'd give it a try. Ready, set, go! Tony swung his ax so hard that a huge hickory tree broke off like a matchstick. Big Bill hired Tony, and that's how Tony got into the lumbering business.

Before long, Tony had figured out how to cut down two trees with one swing. He'd cut down one on the back swing and one on the down swing. Pretty soon he got bored with that and just started pulling trees out by the roots.

Tony Beaver was as famous a logger in West Virginia as his cousin Paul Bunyan was up north. Like Paul, who had Babe the Blue Ox, Tony had two oxen named Hannibal and Goliath.

One time, Tony challenged his cousin Paul to a skating contest. They wrapped slabs of bacon around their skates and raced back and forth, greasing their grandmaw's pancake griddle. Tony won that race, by the way.

Tony Beaver lived a long, successful life and had many great adventures. To this day, they still talk about Tony Beaver in the hills of West Virginia.

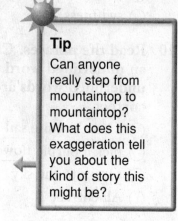

Tip

Can anyone really step from mountaintop to mountaintop? What does this exaggeration tell you about the kind of story this might be?

Tip

Create a mental picture of Tony and Paul skating on their grandmaw's griddle. How big would the griddle have to be?

© Harcourt

Name _____

1 The author's purpose for writing this story was to

○ persuade people to become loggers.

○ entertain readers with a tall tale.

○ explain a process.

○ describe a place.

Tip
Imagine a Venn diagram. Which answer choice belongs in the center of the diagram, under the label "Both"?

2 One way that Tony Beaver and Paul Bunyan are alike is that

○ Paul is Tony's cousin.

○ they are loggers.

○ they are from West Virginia.

○ each has a blue ox named Babe.

3 Which picture shows Hannibal and Goliath?

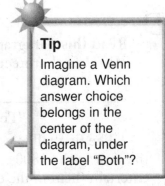

○   ○   ○   ○

4 An example of an exaggeration that makes this story effective is the size of

○ the mountaintops.

○ Tony's ax.

○ the hickory tree.

○ Grandmaw's griddle.

5 Which statement expresses an opinion?

○ Tony had chopped down trees for Paw, so he told Big Bill he'd give it a try.

○ Paw and Maw Beaver lived in a log cabin on top of a hill with the three little Beavers.

○ Even among these pioneers, the Beaver family was unusual.

○ To this day, they still talk about Tony Beaver in the hills of West Virginia.

Tip
The correct answer is the one that tells what someone thinks or feels. An opinion is not a fact, even if many people agree with it, because it cannot be proved.

© Harcourt

Standards: 4-R2.10, 4-R2.11, 4-R1.7, 4-R2.6, 4-R1.13

Directions

Read this paragraph from a report a student wrote about tall tales. It has several mistakes that need correcting. Then answer Questions 6 through 8.

Telling Tall Tales

[1] The first tall tales were told by pioneers who settled the west in the 1800s. [2] Without movies or TV to entertain them in the evenings, people gathered around and told funny stories. [3] Some tall tales were told about real people, such as Johnny Appleseed and Davy Crockett other characters in tall tales were fictional workers. [4] Loggers, cowboys, railroad workers, and steel workers all had there special heroes.

---

6 Which sentence contains two complete thoughts and should be written as two sentences?

○ Sentence 1
○ Sentence 2
○ Sentence 3
○ Sentence 4

Tip
Look for two sentences that should be written as separate sentences or as a compound sentence but are joined incorrectly.

7 Which is the <u>best</u> way to rewrite Sentence 4?

○ Loggers, cowboys, railroad workers, and steel workers all had their special heroes.

○ Loggers, cowboys, railroad workers, and steel workers all had they special heroes.

○ Loggers, cowboys, railroad workers, and steel workers all had them special heroes.

○ Loggers, cowboys, railroad workers, and steel workers all had they're special heroes.

Tip
Read Sentence 4 to identify the error and think of how to correct it. Then pick the answer choice that shows the correct word to replace the word *there*.

8 What is the student's purpose for writing this report?

○ to entertain readers with a tall tale
○ to persuade readers to tell tall tales
○ to tell how to make up a tall tale
○ to explain how tall tales began

Directions

Choose the word or words that correctly complete the sentence.

9 Charlie skates _____ than I do.

○ faster
○ more faster
○ more fast
○ most faster

Tip
When comparing two actions, add -er to most short adverbs. Use *more* before most adverbs of two or more syllables.

10 Choose the words that correctly complete the sentence.

The large bell _____ , but the small bells _____ .

○ clang, jingle
○ clang, jingles
○ clangs, jingle
○ clangs, jingles

11 Read the phrases. Choose the phrase containing an underlined word that is spelled wrong. If all the underlined words are spelled correctly, mark "All correct."

○ carrot seeds
○ spilled milk
○ deliver a package
○ All correct

12 Create an imaginary hero. Write two sentences about your imaginary hero. Check your completed sentences to make sure you capitalized and punctuated correctly.

_____

_____

_____

Standards: 4-W1.5, 4-W1.5, 4-W1.5, 4-W1.5

STOP

Name _____

𝐃irections

Read the poem below. Then answer Questions 1 through 5. You may look back at the poem.

Lizards

Lizards are shy. In fact, most are meek.

Lizards are small, swift, smooth, and sleek.

Whether they're orange, blue, yellow, or green,

Lizards, I think, prefer not to be seen.

Quick as a sneeze, they scurry from sight.

It doesn't take much to give them a fright!

They hide in dark corners where no one can see them,

Although there are some that live in museums.

Even in cages, they hide from our view.

Are you scared of lizards? They're frightened of you!

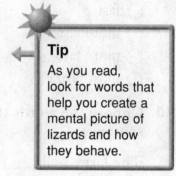

Tip

As you read, look for words that help you create a mental picture of lizards and how they behave.

© Harcourt

1 Which of these statements is <u>not</u> true about the poem?

- ◯ Each pair of lines rhyme.
- ◯ It uses alliteration, or words with similar beginning sounds.
- ◯ The tone of the poem is dark and gloomy.
- ◯ It contains many adjectives that tell about lizards.

2 Which word can help you figure out the meaning of *meek*?

- ◯ *small*
- ◯ *swift*
- ◯ *smooth*
- ◯ *shy*

3 What does the poem mean when it says "Quick as a sneeze, they scurry from sight"?

- ◯ Lizards are frightened by sneezes.
- ◯ Lizards run and hide in as little time as it takes to sneeze.
- ◯ Sneezing helps lizards run faster.
- ◯ Lizards make a sneezing sound to warn each other of danger.

4 Which statement best expresses the poet's opinion?

- ◯ People should not be afraid of lizards.
- ◯ Lizards make great pets.
- ◯ People and lizards are alike in many ways.
- ◯ Lizards are scary creatures.

5 Write one or more sentences that tell how this poem makes you feel.

_____

_____

_____

> **Tip**
> The question asks you to write about your feelings. For example, you might tell about feelings you had as you read the poem or how you feel about lizards as a result of reading the poem.

© Harcourt

Standards: 4-R2.9, 4-R3.4, 4-R3.5, 4-R2.10, 4-R1.16

Directions

Read this paragraph that a student wrote about a helicopter ride. It has several mistakes that need correcting. Then answer Questions 6 through 8.

[1] Today Dennis had a truly unforgettable experience—an exciting helicopter ride. [2] After the helicopter landed. [3] The passengers strolled among spectacular gardens. [4] The fragrance of the flowers fills the air. [5] From the helicopter, Dennis was able to see valleys, cliffs, and waterfalls.

6 Which sentence is incomplete?

- ○ Sentence 1
- ○ Sentence 2
- ○ Sentence 3
- ○ Sentence 4

7 Which is the best way to rewrite Sentence 4?

- ○ The fragrance of the flowers fill the air.
- ○ The fragrance of the flowers filling the air.
- ○ The fragrance of the flowers filled the air.
- ○ The fragrance of the flowers has filled the air.

Tip
Think about the tense in which the rest of the paragraph is written to choose the correct tense of the verb.

8 Rewrite sentence 5 so that it is more descriptive. Use precise words that help the reader picture what you are describing.

_____

_____

_____

© Harcourt

Standards: 4-W1.5, 4-W1.5, 4-W1.4

Directions

Look at the underlined part of the sentence. Choose the answer that shows the correct capitalization for that part. If the underlined part is correct, mark "Correct as is."

Tip
Take time to look carefully at the title. Be sure that each word that needs to be capitalized is capitalized in your answer choice.

9 "Strange Plants <u>Of the Rain Forest</u>" is the name of <u>a magazine article I'm reading.</u>

○ "Strange plants of the Rain Forest"
○ "Strange Plants Of The Rain Forest"
○ "Strange Plants of the Rain Forest"
○ Correct as is

10 Choose the word that correctly completes the sentence.

Please sit beside _____.

○ I
○ me
○ myself
○ my

Tip
The word *beside* is a preposition. What form of the pronoun should follow the preposition?

11 Choose the word that is spelled correctly and completes the sentence.

Mom said this was her _____ warning to clean my room.

○ finnal
○ finell
○ finale
○ final

12 Write a sentence about a good hiding place for a small animal or other creature. Check your finished sentence for correct grammar and spelling.

_____

_____

_____

Directions

Read the story below. Then answer Questions 1 through 5. You may look back at the story.

The Online Museum

Nira frowned at the computer screen and sighed. Her brother Miko sighed, too. He loved using the computer, but it was Nira's turn. He was trying to read his history lesson while he waited, but it wasn't easy. Nira sighed again, louder this time.

"Okay, what is it?" Miko asked.

"We're supposed to go to a museum this weekend and write a report about it," Nira said. "I can't go Saturday because of my soccer game. I was doing a search for a museum that's open on Sunday, but I can't find one. So, I don't know what to do."

Miko said, "I know what you can do, but you have to let me get on the computer."

"It's my turn, though," Nira complained.

"Come on!" Miko insisted. "You don't even like using the computer."

"Well, all right," Nira said. "It just takes so long." She slid over and let Miko sit at the keyboard. He made a few clicks with the mouse and then turned the monitor so that it faced her.

"There," he said. A brightly colored picture of a Sioux chief filled the screen. Next to the picture was information about the painter and the painting. "It's the art museum in the city," Miko said. "You can find all sorts of information and see paintings and items from all the collections."

"Is it really the museum?" Nira asked.

"Sure it is," Miko said. "Part of the exhibit is online. Have fun, click with the mouse, and look around. Don't worry. You'll be able to write the best report in class. You might even get extra credit for being the only student to visit an online museum!"

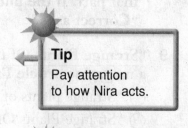

Tip
Pay attention to how Nira acts.

Tip
In this paragraph, Nira explains her problem. You need to identify the problem in a story in order to understand the plot.

1 **At the beginning of the story, Nira feels**

   ○ delighted.

   ○ annoyed.

   ○ sorrowful.

   ○ hopeful.

> **Tip**
> The story does not say how Nira feels, but you can figure it out from her actions at the beginning of the story and from your own experience.

2 **If you did not know the meaning of the word** *insisted*, **where could you find its definition?**

   ○ an atlas

   ○ a dictionary

   ○ an encyclopedia

   ○ a thesaurus

3 **In addition to the main purpose of entertaining readers, the author may also have wanted to**

   ○ give directions for doing a computer search.

   ○ give information about museums.

   ○ advertise the online museum.

   ○ persuade readers to take advantage of online resources.

4 **Which sentence best expresses the author's perspective?**

   ○ Online museums are better than real ones.

   ○ Students should spend less time on the computer.

   ○ The computer can be a helpful tool for students.

   ○ Visiting museums is a waste of time.

> **Tip**
> The author's perspective is his or her opinion about a subject. Determine the author's perspective by thinking about the details and language he or she used in the story.

5 **Write one or more sentences to identify the problem Nira has in the story and tell how it is resolved.**

_____

_____

_____

_____

Standards: 4-R2.1, 4-R3.1, 4-R2.10, 4-R2.5, 4-R2.2

Directions

Read this topic sentence that a student wrote for the first draft of a report on a famous museum. Then answer Questions 6 through 8.

When architect Frank Lloyd Wright designed the building that would hold the Guggenheim Museum, he looked to nature.

6 **Choose the sentences that best develop the topic sentence.**

○ A recent exhibit on motorcycles was especially popular. Millions of visitors flocked to the museum to see it.

○ The museum resembles the spiral shell of a sea animal called the nautilus. The main exhibition hall is built in the shape of a spiral.

○ The Guggenheim Museum is located in New York City. It opened in 1959.

○ Frank Lloyd Wright designed other famous buildings, too. He is regarded as one of the outstanding architects of his time.

Tip

All of the choices tell something about the Guggenheim Museum or about Frank Lloyd Wright. The correct choice is the detail that gives more information about the main idea expressed in the topic sentence.

7 **Which resource would be most likely to give useful information on this topic?**

○ a dictionary

○ an encyclopedia

○ an atlas

○ a thesaurus

8 **For what purpose would this report be written?**

○ to entertain readers with an interesting story

○ to give information about the life of Frank Lloyd Wright

○ to describe the structure of the Guggenheim Museum

○ to persuade readers to visit the museum

Tip

Reports most frequently are written to gather and share information.

© Harcourt

Standards: 4-W1.3, 4-RS2.1, 4-R2.10

Time to Write

*D*irections

Write one or more paragraphs about why it is important to follow directions. Tell what might happen if you did not follow directions. Include examples to make your point clear.

Writer's Checklist

Remember to:

❏ Write about why it is important to follow directions.

❏ Use specific details to support your response.

❏ Include a variety of sentence types.

❏ Use interesting words and phrases.

❏ Organize your response in a clear and logical way.

❏ Use complete sentences.

❏ Write clearly and neatly.

❏ Use correct punctuation, capitalization, and spelling, and correct any errors you find.

Standards: 4-W1.2, 4-W1.3, 4-W1.5, 4-W1.6.1, 4-W2.1

STOP